THROUGH THE EYES OF N.T. WRIGHT

A READER'S GUIDE TO *PAUL AND THE FAITHFULNESS OF GOD*

DEREK VREELAND

Through the Eyes of N. T. Wright:
A Reader's Guide to Paul
and the Faithfulness of God

Published by Doctrina Press

Printed in the United States of America

Cover and interior design by IndieDesignz.com

ISBN-13: 978-0692455838

ISBN-10: 0692455833

"N. T. Wright is a rare theologian, whose work must be grappled with seriously. But few pastors have the time or the tools necessary to do so. Yet, relying on video clips or online summaries and critiques simply won't do. Derek Vreeland has given us a gift. As a pastor and a scholar, Vreeland has carefully worked his way through Wright's magnum opus and synopsized it in a clear and readable way. Employing precise yet jargon-free language, Vreeland has given us a gateway into Wright's world, a world where the stunning faithfulness of God is revealed in Jesus Christ."

— GLENN PACKIAM, *Lead Pastor, New Life Downtown, Colorado Springs, Colorado*

"The best result of Derek Vreeland's summaries of the magisterial work of N. T. Wright, *Paul and the Faithfulness of God*, will be when readers read Derek with a view to dipping here and there for long spells in Wright's own book. Wright's book on Paul is very, very long — and probably too long for many who most need it — but the prose is accessible and the insights remarkable so this summary of *Paul and the Faithfulness of God* will open up the fullness of this new vision of the apostle Paul. I commend Derek's work because I commend Wright's work."

— SCOT MCKNIGHT, *Professor of New Testament, Northern Seminary, Lombard, Illinois*

"Derek Vreeland has rendered us a great service. N. T. Wright is the most respected New Testament scholar of our era and his work on the theology of Paul could not be more important. But the fact remains that many are not up to the task of wading through 1,700 pages of dense scholarship. Derek Vreeland's reader's guide is an excellent distillation of Paul and the Faithfulness of God and thus a true gift."

— BRIAN ZAHND, *Lead Pastor, Word of Life Church, St. Joseph, Missouri*

"N. T. Wright's two-volume work on Paul is nothing less than mountainous—hugely formidable and intimidating. So, even those already familiar with Wrightian terrain can be glad for a guide, especially one as capable as Derek Vreeland. In this introduction, Vreeland thankfully does not restate Wright in simpler, briefer terms; instead, he identifies decisive concepts and themes and explains in his own words their significance for Wright's larger project. The result is a work that not only provides access to the height, depth, and width of Wright's work on Paul, but also draws us into fresh engagements with the sacred Scriptures themselves."
— CHRIS GREEN, *Assistant Professor of Theology, Pentecostal Seminary, Cleveland, Tennessee*

"I often ask my friends what theologians will be remembered, 500 years from now, as the dominant voices of our era. I am convinced that N. T. Wright will stand at the top of that list. Whether you agree with him, or disagree, his influence is difficult to challenge. In this concise book, my friend Derek Vreeland has provided a genuine resource to help today's church parse the words and theology of Wright. Even though I generally love Wright's teaching, I do find a few areas of disagreement with his view of Pauline theology. Regardless, even in disagreement, the study of Wright is vital for all contemporary theologians and Vreeland has done the church a service by making Wright's theology more accessible for every believer. You should read this book."
— MICAH FRIES, *Vice President of LifeWay Research, LifeWay Christian Resources, Nashville, Tennessee*

Contents

PREFACE

N. T. Wright has given the church a great gift. This gift arrived in my mailbox in November 2013. I remember tearing open the brown cardboard box with great anticipation. Under the packing slip sat this beautiful gift in two large paperback volumes —*Paul and the Faithfulness of God*, the long awaited big book on the theology of Paul. N. T. "Tom" Wright has been the most influential theological voice in my ear for quite some time. I had already read a number of his books including two of the three academic books in the "Christian Origins and the Question of God" series. I had read *Jesus and the Victory of God* and *The Resurrection of the Son of God*, parts 2 and 3 in the series, and I had been waiting for years for part 4 to be released. (I have not read *The New Testament and the People of God*, the first part of this series, and I still feel a measure of guilt for not having done so, especially when Wright mentions it so often in the early parts of *Paul and the Faithfulness of God*. Hopefully, I will get to it one day.) The books in this series are indeed academic books written for an academic audience. By "academic" I mean they are filled with technical language, big complex theological terms, and numerous footnotes and citations. Part of the work in writing an academic book is demonstrating one's familiarity with other books written on the same subject and a willingness to compare and contrast one's own view against the views of other scholars. The list of books and articles written by other scholars and referenced by Wright in the writing of *Paul and the Faithfulness of God* is itself 70 pages. He tacks on that list at the end of the second volume bringing the total page count of the two-volume book to nearly 1,700 pages.

Paul and the Faithfulness of God, or the "big book on Paul," is a tremendous gift not only to the academic world, but to the church, to me and you, to the average Christian attending church in an ordinary town in North America. Wright has given us a fresh look at the writings, and specifically the theology, of the chief apostolic, Spirit-inspired writer of the New Testament. Wright's interpretation of Paul challenges how some Christians have read Paul, but it is a challenge offered from a place of deep respect for the historical context in which Paul was writing. In a world of pragmatic Bible application where "what does the Bible mean to me?" still exists, Wright helps us reread the Spirit-inspired apostle from Paul's perspective in his historical context. In other words, Wright rescues Paul from falling victim to private, individual, modern interpretations, allowing us to hear what he had to say when he wrote under the inspiration of the Holy Spirit nearly 2,000 years ago.

Wright has interpreted Paul for us. I want to sum up Wright for you.

I started reading *Paul and the Faithfulness of God* on the First Sunday of Advent in December 2013. My goal was to finish the entire book, both volumes, five months later on Easter Sunday 2014. I created a reading schedule where I assigned myself daily reading for six days a week, keeping Sundays open as a catch up day. My reading schedule had me wrapping up the book during Holy Week. The plan was great; my discipline to stick to the plan was not equally as great. I fell behind and by the time Easter rolled around I was in the final section, but still 180 pages from the finish line. I didn't reach my goal of finishing the book by Easter, but in March

2014 I had the opportunity to hear Wright lecture at St. Mellitus Theological Centre at Christ Church Anglican in Kansas City. It was my first time listening to him lecture live-in-person and, honestly, I was as excited as a 12 year-old girl at a One Direction concert. I had the opportunity to speak to him briefly after his morning lecture, snap a quick picture, and have him sign my copy of *Paul and the Faithfulness of God*. I wish I would have had more time to talk to him, but I did thank him for his work and for serving as my theological mentor. I moved on to read other things after Easter including Wright's *Surprised by Scripture*, a collection of essays and lectures on the role of scripture in current contemporary discussions. During the summer of 2014, I began to go through the book a second time in order to create an outline of the book for a class I wanted to teach at our church. I had never tried to teach a theological book in a classroom setting for members of my church before then. I announced the class and had a sign-up sheet in our church foyer and to my amazement about 15 people signed up for the class.

I ended up breaking the book into nine parts and I presented each part on Sunday nights for nine weeks in a class I entitled "N. T. Wright and the Faithfulness of Paul." I prepared a five-page outline for each class session and I was shocked to see people return week after week eager to participate. I am indebted to the members from Word of Life Church who attended the class. The outlines I prepared for them have become the reader's guide I have written for you. I believe *Paul and the Faithfulness of God* is a massively important book, but its size and academic tone will make it inaccessible for many people who love Jesus, love the church, love the scriptures, and want to understand what Paul meant in his many letters. I sincerely believe Wright wants his work to affect the life of the church, so I am happy to help in bridging the gap between the academic world and the church world.

As I was finishing up the preparation of the outlines, I was able to finish reading the last 180 pages of the book. I finished the final outline, part nine of my nine-week class, the night before the last class. I intended on editing the outlines and making them available for people who wanted to see my complete notes on the book. As I compiled the outlines, I found them to be long enough to go through another round of editing into a manuscript that could be published as a paperback book and e-book and now, here it is. I offer this reader's guide for all those who would like help in understanding Wright's book so they can grow in their understanding of Paul's books in the New Testament. I have spent over a year reading, thinking, teaching, and writing about Wright's big book on Paul and the result is this condensed reader's guide. I am thankful for Barbara Young for proofreading the manuscript. Her keen eye and helpful comments have made this project better than it was in its first draft. I am also indebted to Fortress Press in the US and SPCK Publishing in the UK for granting me permission to quote heavily from Wright in this reader's guide. Finally, I am grateful for Tom Wright and his tireless effort to serve the church by challenging us to engage with the church's sacred texts with serious attention to the historical context, so we can hear what Jesus and Paul have to say to us today.

Space does not allow, especially in a short book like this one, to outline all of the intricate arguments and points Wright makes in his book. I have worked through the big book on Paul to bring to light the important conclusions and contributions Wright has to offer to the church concerning the theology of Paul. Often I summarize Wright's thoughts into my own words, but frequently I quote directly from him. All quotations from Wright in this reader's guide are in italics. I have highlighted some of Wright's specific treatments of key Bible passages to show how he arrived at some of his conclusions. I do not highlight all of the key biblical texts he interacts with in forming these conclusions. For example, he may have cited five different Bible passages as evidence for a certain point he is trying to make and I chose just one passage to show Wright's work with the text. I do provide a more complete overview of Wright's vision of

Paul's understanding of justification in multiple passages because Wright seems to be questioned often regarding his views on justification in Paul's letters.

While you can read my book and have a general understanding of Wright's primary conclusions in his book, this reader's guide does not replace reading the book itself. In this regard, I serve as an interpretive editor picking and choosing what I consider to be the most important theological conclusions drawn by Wright in his big book on Paul, while only providing brief remarks on the biblical and historical evidence Wright supplies. For example, I do not give adequate space in the beginning or the end of this reader's guide to cover all the depth of material Wright provides to layout Paul's historical context which is an undeniably critical component to the evidence Wright offers to defend his conclusions regarding Paul's theology. I freely admit in creating a guide like this one, I may indeed miss important contributions still hidden away in Wright's book. Nevertheless, I am confident the book I have written will serve as a worthy introduction to many of the important themes in Paul's theology. If we prayerfully think through the implications of the themes provided by Wright, I believe our faith will grow, our hope will soar, and our love for God and the church will deepen and mature.

Almighty God, you have given your only-begotten Son to take our nature upon him, and to be born of a pure virgin: Grant that we, who have been born again and made your children by adoption and grace, may daily be renewed by your Holy Spirit; through our Lord Jesus Christ, to whom with you and the same Spirit be honor and glory, now and for ever. Amen.

Derek Vreeland
Christmas Day 2014

INTRODUCING N. T. WRIGHT AND THE BIG BOOK ON PAUL

Paul and the Faithfulness of God, Chapter 1

N. T. Wright is arguably the most important theological voice in the church today. He may, in fact, be saving evangelical faith. In the cover story of the April 2014 issue of Christianity Today, United Methodist Pastor Jason Byassee wrote, "(Wright) is the most prolific biblical scholar in a generation. Some say he is the most important apologist for the Christian faith since C. S. Lewis. He has written the most extensive series of popular commentaries on the New Testament since William Barclay. In case three careers sound like too few, he is also a church leader, having served as Bishop of Durham, England before his current teaching post at the University of St. Andrews in Scotland. But perhaps the most significant praise of all: When Wright speaks, preaches, or writes, folks say they see

Jesus, and lives are transformed."[1] While numerous theological questions have been raised by those within evangelicalism creating a bit of uncertainty for the movement, N. T. Wright has become a stabilizing force, and indeed for many, a needed catalyst for theological shifts towards a more authentic, historically-rich faith. I admit I am not the most objective reader of Wright. I have found his interpretation of Paul and his theological arguments so compelling that I have thrown up my hands and said, "You win." I consider him to be my primary theology mentor because in him I see Jesus and a love for the church and I am not the only one. I see his saving acts within my own non-denominational tribe, but his influence seemingly has no bounds. It seems like everyone is reading N. T. Wright. I know Pentecostals, Evangelicals, Baptists (even Reformed Baptists!), Methodists, Disciples of Christ, Presbyterians, Mennonites, Lutherans, and his native Anglicans who are all reading and wrestling with this theological heavyweight.

N. T. Wright's Career

Wright received his training at Oxford, completing his doctoral dissertation on the book of Romans. He lectured in Canada and back at Oxford before serving as Bishop of Durham, a prestigious position within the Church of England. The bishop has oversight over quite a number of parish churches and serves as a member of the House of Lords in the British parliament. In 2010, Wright left his post with the church to return to the university. He is currently the Research Professor of New Testament and Early Christianity at St. Andrews in Scotland. He continues to write and lecture both in the UK and in North America. He has published nearly 50 books, written a complete New Testament commentary series (*The New Testament for Everyone*),

[1] Jason Byassee, "Surprised by Wright," *Christianity Today*, April, 2014, 36

completed an original translation of the New Testament, and written numerous articles, essays, lectures, and sermons. With over 40 years of ministry and academic work, he has spent his career focusing on themes related to Jesus, the gospels, and Paul. He writes from the perspective of a historian, paying very close attention to the historical context of the biblical writers. He is highly regarded as the most important New Testament scholar in the world. As a lover of the church and her mission, many see him as leaving a legacy as influential and widespread as C. S. Lewis or Karl Barth.

The Big Book on Paul

Wright's *magnum opus*, his greatest work, his masterpiece, is *Paul and the Faithfulness of God,* affectionately known by many of his readers and admirers as the "big book on Paul." This book is the fourth in a series of scholarly books on Christian origins. Towards the end of the book, Wright discloses the topic of the upcoming fifth book in the series—the mission of the church. There seems to be an orderly progression in the books in this series. First a book on the New Testament itself, then a book on Jesus, followed by a book on the resurrection of Jesus, then a book on Paul's theology, answering questions like: What did Paul believe about God? How did he think about the nature of the people of God? What was his view of the future for God's world?

One of the helpful tools in navigating through a book as big and complex as *Paul and the Faithfulness of God* is to divide the book into manageable parts and create a roadmap so we do not get lost as we follow the author through all the twists and turns and side-road excursions he takes us on. Wright himself divides the book into four parts:

1. Paul's World (historical context)
2. Paul's Mindset (an understanding of his worldview)

3. Paul's Theology (what he believed)
4. Paul in History (how his theology contrasted with the worlds he lived in)

The densest part of *Paul and the Faithfulness of God* is Wright's discussion of Paul's theology, the third part of the book. I have broken this substantial third section into three individual chapters in the readers guide to give adequate space for Wright's discussion of God, God's people, and God's future — three predominant themes in Paul's theology. I have created the following outline to lead you through Wright's big book:

Chapter 2 — Birds in Paul's Head
+ Life in a Jewish world
+ Ancient philosophy in a Greek world
+ First-century empire in a Roman world

Chapter 3 — Paul's Worldview
+ The convergence of his three worlds
+ Worldview as defined by four distinct, but interrelated, cultural elements active in his day: praxis (common practices), symbols, stories, and questions

Chapter 4 — God: Monotheism Rethought
+ What does it mean for the God of Israel to be one?
+ How does the coming of Jesus and the outpouring of the Spirit change his view of the one God?

Chapter 5 — God's People: Election Redefined
+ Who are the covenant-people of God?
+ How does the inclusion of Gentiles change the nature of God's chosen people?

A Little Window

Wright started in a good place in his exploration of Paul's theology, but where he begins may be surprising to some; he starts with the apostle's shortest epistle, his letter to his friend, Philemon. Onesimus was a slave in the home of Philemon. Apparently, he had fled from his place of duty and ventured out into the city of Rome. There he met Paul and became a Christian. Wright describes Onesimus more as a wandering slave than a runaway slave, because "runaway" denotes more defiance in Onesimus than was probably there. While Paul was under house arrest in Rome, he wrote a letter to Philemon asking him to take Onesimus back, not as a slave, but as a "beloved brother."[2] The letter concludes with a cliffhanger. We do not know exactly how the story ends. The traditional story is that Onesimus does return to the home of Philemon, but then is sent back to Paul where he received training from him before Paul's death. According to Eastern Orthodox tradition, Onesimus became a leader in the early church and eventually the bishop of Ephesus. This story in Paul's apostolic ministry is a peek into key concepts

[2] Philemon 1:16

throughout his other letters: reconciliation, unity, and partnership through Jesus the Christ, the Jewish Messiah. This short letter to Philemon captures one of the dominant themes of his theology. According to Wright, "*Paul's Jewish worldview, radically reshaped around the crucified Messiah, challenges the world of ancient paganism with the concrete signs of the faithfulness of God. That is a summary both of the letter to Philemon and of the entire present book.*"[3] What motivated Philemon and Onesimus to reconcile as history and tradition tells us they did? They reconciled because they were living under the reign of God, where they saw his nature demonstrated in acts of reconciliation and forgiveness.

Worldview and Theology

The bulk of *Paul and the Faithfulness of God* is a fresh reading of the theology of Paul under three themes: monotheism, election, and eschatology. His theology (what he believed about God and God's world) was dependent upon, and shaped by, his worldview (how he saw the world). Theology is what a person believes. Worldview is how a person sees, or more importantly, worldview shapes how a person sees. In this regard, worldview is a person's perspective, his or her point of view, the interpretive lens by which people consciously and more often than not, unconsciously interpret and evaluate the world around them. A worldview is like a pair of glasses. Those of us who wear glasses do not spend much time looking at our glasses; we look through them. They cause what we look at to come into focus. I am nearsighted. Without my glasses everything in the distance is fuzzy. The further an object is from me, the more blurry it becomes. When I look through my prescription glasses, objects in the distance come into focus. Objects are not actually blurry, but

[3] Wright, *Paul and the Faithfulness of God*, 21

they look blurry without my glasses. Wearing glasses with the right prescription allows me to see things as they are intended to look. A worldview is similar. If theology is what Paul is looking at, then his worldview is what he is looking through. If his theology seems fuzzy to a reader, then that reader needs to put on Paul's worldview, only then will his theology come into sharp focus. Attempting to grapple with Paul's theology without knowledge of his worldview is a sure way of misunderstanding him.

What is at the heart of Paul's theology? For the Protestant reformers, the heart of his theology was justification by faith in the context of salvation. Other themes in his writings were tangential and peripheral. Wright challenges not only the centrality of justification by faith in his theology, but challenges the reformed (Lutheran and Calvinistic) interpretations of Paul. This challenge has been called the "New Perspective." While there are many "new perspectives," Wright has become the leading voice in this so-called "new" way of reading Paul. The title is a bit of a misnomer. Those of the new perspective would claim their reading of Paul is closer to an ancient reading of the Apostle, as it is working with his writings in his historical context, making the "new perspective" older than the "old perspective." What I am calling the "Old Perspective" is the dominant interpretation growing out of the Protestant Reformation, which itself does not have a single voice. Leaders in the Protestant Reformation did not always agree on their interpretation of Paul. While the line of demarcation between these two perspectives is often unclear, you can see these two positions in contrast on a number of key issues related to interpreting his theology.[4]

---

[4] To see the contrast of these perspectives over the doctrine of justification, see John Piper, *The Future of Justification: A Response to N. T. Wright*, Wheaton, IL: Crossway, 2007 and N. T. Wright, *Justification: God's Plan & Paul's Vision*, Downers Grove, IL: InterVarsity Press, 2009.

"New Perspective"	"Old Perspective"
Paul's theology is driven by ecclesiology.	Paul's theology is driven by soteriology.
Justification is both juridical and participatory.	Justification is primarily juridical.
Justification is the declaration of membership in God's covenant family.	Justification is the declaration of a right relationship with God.
Judaism was a religion of grace.	Judaism was a religion of legalism.
Paul redefines Jewish thought/categories.	Paul rejects Jewish thought/categories.
Righteousness is "covenant faithfulness."	Righteousness is a moral quality or legal standing.
God's righteousness is his faithfulness to his covenant with Abraham.	God's righteousness is his moral integrity.
We embody God's righteousness.	We receive the imputation of Christ's righteousness.
The gospel is the proclamation of Christ's lordship through his death, resurrection, and ascension.	The gospel is the proclamation of justification by faith through grace communicated through the shed blood of Jesus Christ.

Wright as a contributor to the so-called "new perspective" on Paul uses three primary tools in understanding his theology. First he uses history. This tool is a natural starting point, because if we want to see what he meant when he wrote what he did, we need to step back and look at Paul in his historical context. Language only makes sense when it is given proper definition in its given cultural setting. The meaning of words change over time as a culture itself changes and grows. For example, fifty years ago the word "rap" was a verb meaning to knock repeatedly on a hard service. It is what people did when they stood outside the front door of your house. They would *rap* on the door. Today in popular speech the word refers to a specific genre of music. Context is essential if we are to understand the meaning of language, so Wright starts with Paul in the setting of "second temple Judaism," a term Wright uses to describe the period of time when the Temple was rebuilt during the exile until the destruction of the Temple by the Romans in 70 AD. This period of second temple Judaism was filled with Jewish, Roman, and Greek influences.

The second tool Wright uses is what scholars call "exegesis," that is, the translation of Scripture from their original languages into English. Paul wrote in the Greek language and without advanced training in ancient Greek, we are dependent upon scholars to translate his writings into English. While historical context is the first step to understanding him, it only sets the stage to understand what the Greek words he wrote mean in modern-day English. The final tool Wright uses is "application" or "relevance," that is, understanding how hearers in Paul's day would have understood the meaning of the words he used. These three tools work together and are essential in understanding his theology. If we do not know what he meant in his historical setting, then we are unable to translate the words he used from Greek to English in a way that would have made sense to his original audience.

Standing behind Paul's theology is his worldview, his way of looking at the world. In order to determine his worldview, Wright examines four cultural elements of Paul's historical context. The first element in forming his worldview is *praxis*, the question Wright is asking is: "What were the common practices in his world?" Wright will be looking at the activities, the rituals, the lived-out habits of people living in Paul's day. The second cultural element is *symbol* with the question: "What key symbols filled Paul's world?" Symbols include artifacts of culture such as language, art, architecture, etc. The third element is *story* in which Wright asks: "What narratives shaped Paul's imagination?" These are not merely the stories told for entertainment, but the big stories shaping the culture of his world. Often we call these "framing narratives," because they are big stories that give shape and meaning to a culture. In our modern American context we can think of the stories of George Washington and Valley Forge or Abraham Lincoln and the Gettysburg Address as framing narratives for American culture. Finally, Wright looks at *questions* as an element in determining Paul's worldview, asking: "What were the big questions people were asking in his world?" Determining the important questions people were asking helps to uncover popular cultural values and priorities influencing his point of view.

Theology and worldview work together, but they are not the same thing. The work of theology forms our core beliefs about God, his world, and the people he has created. Worldview is the way we look at the world, how we assign value to things or people, how we prioritize, categorize, and give meaning to what we observe. Theology is the collection of the constructed evaluations we have made or accepted based on our worldview. Theology is conscious; worldview is more often subconscious. Theology is the evaluation of what we are looking at. Worldview is what we are looking through. Understanding how these two relate to each other is a necessary first step in making sense of Paul's letters.

CHAPTER 2

BIRDS IN PAUL'S HEAD

Paul and the Faithfulness of God, Chapters 2-5

We are headed towards an exploration of Paul's theology, a collection of core beliefs shaping the very foundation of the church in which you and I participate. Before we can dive headlong into his theology, we must look into his mind to understand his worldview, and before we can understand his worldview, we must look to the past, into the world where he lived. Paul's world was complex and we are at a disadvantage. He lived nearly 2,000 years ago and we have very few historical records to establish what life was like in the ancient world. From the material historians like Wright have reviewed, we can see Paul lived in the overlap of three worlds at once. Paul lived and preached in a Jewish world, a Greek world, and a Roman world.

These three worlds are both distinct and interrelated. We can identify clear values and cultural markers for each world making each unique, but they were deeply intertwined and alive in Paul's imagination and thoughts. These worlds shaped Paul's worldview.

Wright uses a four-fold criteria in examining the worldviews in each of these worlds by asking questions such as:

1. What were the common practices? (praxis)
2. What were the key symbols? (symbol)
3. What narratives shaped the culture? (story)
4. What were the big, important questions people were asking? (question)

In looking at Paul's historical context by piecing together the worldview of each world, we will be able to reconstruct Paul's own worldview. Wright uses various bird metaphors to describe the uniqueness of each world. He calls the Jewish world the "hovering birds" and the Greek world the "owl of Athene." He uses the metaphor of the "rooster for Asclepius" to describe the world of pagan religion and the "landing eagle" to represent the Roman Empire.

Hovering Birds: The Jewish World

To describe Paul's Jewish world, he does not attempt to reconstruct a massive overview of Israel's history leading up to the first century experience of the Jewish people. He does not attempt an all-encompassing review of the complexity of the Jewish worldview of Paul's day. Rather Wright is content with doing one thing: "*I hope in particular to bring out the way in which the faithfulness of Israel's God functions as a theme throughout so much of the period.*"[1] The emphasis Wright makes in Paul's theology is the theme of the faithfulness of God, so he shines the light on Paul's Jewish context to highlight the predominance of the theme of faithfulness.

---

[1] Wright, 77

The Pharisees

A look into Paul's Jewish world starts with a look at the group with whom Jesus had so many encounters—the Pharisees. While there were many different schools of thought in the first-century Jewish world, Paul found himself among the Pharisees. They were a popular and influential movement of Jews in the first century concerned with religious, civic, and social purity, not in terms of personal holiness, but as a sign of loyalty to Israel and to Israel's God. For example, the kosher laws regarding which foods were clean and acceptable to eat was not a matter of individuals demonstrating their own personal faith, but it was a sign to the larger society, and to themselves, that they were faithful to follow through with their responsibilities to the covenant God had made with them. The heart of a Pharisee's life was prayer, rooted in the ancient Jewish *Shema*, the foundational creed-like prayer found in Deuteronomy: "Hear, O Israel: The Lord our God, the Lord is one. You shall love the Lord your God with all your heart and with all your soul and with all your might."[2] To pray the *Shema* allowed Jewish people to confess their faith in the one God of Israel.

The Pharisees were a kingdom-of-God movement. Their zeal for God's kingdom put them at odds with the expansive kingdom of the Roman Empire. The kingdom of God in the mind of a Pharisee was the rule of God upon the earth. This kingdom was not merely a religious rule, as if God was ruling the private "spiritual life" of his people. The kingdom of God for first-century Pharisees was the political rule of God over all the affairs of God's people. Pharisees were zealous for the kingdom. Zeal did not mean they were merely emotionally passionate to see the coming of the kingdom. Rather it meant they were prepared to enter into a holy war as instruments of

[2] Deuteronomy 6:4-5

the reign of Israel's God. To be zealous implied one had a wholehearted-devotion for the kingdom of God, but it also included the willingness to become violent in order to promote the kingdom, much like the violent Jewish Maccabean revolt during the second century BC. As a Pharisee, Paul himself was prone to violent zealotry. He wrote: "I am a Jew, born in Tarsus in Cilicia, but brought up in this city, educated at the feet of Gamaliel according to the strict manner of the law of our fathers, being zealous for God as all of you are this day."[3] While Paul did not often use kingdom-of-God-language in his writings, his roots were firmly planted in this particular Jewish soil saturated with the expectation of the coming of the kingdom of God.

Jewish Symbols-in-Action

Two primary symbols in Paul's Jewish world were the Jewish law (i.e. Torah) and the Jewish Temple. Both of these symbols included key practices, making the Torah and the Temple symbols-in-action, connecting both praxis and symbol in a Jewish worldview. Temple served as a powerful symbol in Jewish imagination, but it was not just the building itself, but the precise ways in which a faithful Jew would participate in the life of the Temple. The Torah was a visible symbol. It was designed to form Israel into a distinct people separate from the pagan Gentile nations. For example, it contains strict laws regarding what the Jews were supposed to eat and with whom they were to share their table. The Temple, as a building, and the Torah, as a collection of scrolls, formed powerful symbols in themselves. They also shaped the core practices of Jewish worship and life.

---

[3] Acts 22:3

According to Wright, *"The Temple in Jerusalem was the focus of the whole Jewish way of life. A good deal of Torah was about what to do in the Temple, and the practice of Torah...itself could be thought of in terms of gaining, at a distance, the blessings you would gain if you were actually there—the blessing, in other words, of the sacred presence itself, the Shekinah, the glory which supposedly dwelt in the Temple but would also dwell 'where two or three study Torah'."*[4] The Temple was the place where heaven and earth met. The hope sustained by Israel's prayer life was the picture of Yahweh, the one God of Israel, dwelling once again in the Temple.[5] Various Psalm-writers expressed this desire for the God of Israel to come once again and dwell in the Temple. For example: "O God, you are my God; earnestly I seek you; my soul thirsts for you; my flesh faints for you, as in a dry and weary land where there is no water. So I have looked upon you in the sanctuary, beholding your power and glory."[6] The Temple served as the point on earth where God made his presence known and therefore the Temple stood as a small picture of the entire creation. God made the earth to be his dwelling place. The expectation of the return of Yahweh to the Temple points to new creation, where God will dwell with his people forever.[7] The symbols of *"temple, presence, glory, kingship, wisdom, creation, exile, rebuilding, and unfulfilled promise —would be part of (first century Jewish) mental and emotional furniture."*[8]

---

[4] Wright, 95

[5] "Yahweh" is the personal name for the God of Israel. It is translated in English Bible as "the LORD."

[6] Psalm 63:1-2

[7] Revelation 21:3

[8] Wright, 107

Jewish Questions and Stories

Many Jewish people of the first century felt like they were participants in an epic story of creation and covenant, but they felt like captives awaiting rescue and the climactic conclusion to their story. They were asking things like, "Since we are still captives under yet another oppressive pagan empire, when will God come to liberate us? When will Yahweh return to the Temple? How could our God, the creator God, not act at last to fulfill his promises?" Jews like the Pharisees, were not looking to the Torah or the Temple asking, "What must we do to go to heaven when we die? How do we earn God's favor so in the afterlife we can avert God's anger? How can we each have an individual, personal relationship with God?" They were asking, "When will Yahweh come rescue us, renew the covenant, and thus rescue the entire world?"

The Old Testament, the first section of our Christian Bible, contains a lot of different kinds of writing. There we find history, lists of commands, prayers, songs, wisdom sayings, and prophecy which reads like poetry. While there are many different voices in the Old Testament, it tells one story, the story of Israel. Wright explains, *"The (Hebrew) Bible was not merely a source of types, shadows, allusions, echoes, symbols, examples, role-models and other no doubt important things. It was all those, but it was much, much more. It presented itself as a single, sprawling, complex but essentially coherent narrative, a narrative still in search of an ending."* As a "coherent narrative" the story of Israel is a complete story with twists and turns that all go together pointing the reader and worshipper of the God of Israel in a certain direction. While the story is coherent in that it is told in a logical way, it remains a story without an ending. Major portions of the story of Israel are told and retold throughout

---

[9] Wright, 116

the Old Testament and this tradition was carried on by Paul and other New Testament characters. Peter's sermon on the Day of Pentecost, Stephen's sermon before his stoning, and Paul's letter to the Romans and Galatians includes a retelling of the story of Israel. While the Old Testament closes without a proper ending, the prophets began to look forward to their story's conclusion, the coming of Messiah, the Jewish king. There is no one single picture of what Messiah would look like according to the prophets, but in many of the retellings of the story of Israel one thing is consistent: there was a longing and waiting for Messiah to come and make things right.

The Jews of Paul's day were living in their ancestral homeland after the Babylonian/Persian exile but the presence of the dominating Roman Empire made them feel as if they were still exiles. Many Jews determined they were still in exile from studying the Torah and seeing Israel's lack of faithfulness to the covenant. Groups like the Pharisees were encouraging strict adherence to the Torah so the God of Israel would come save them and set them free from their captivity. The second-temple Jewish understanding of salvation was not "other-worldly" (i.e. going to heaven after death). Their view of salvation was earth-bound. They wanted to be saved from Roman oppression, saved from sin, primarily the sins of idolatry and injustice, in order to be the agency through which God would do his work of saving the world. Wright describes this as God's restorative justice: "*The rescue of human beings from sin and death, which remains vital throughout, serves a much larger purpose, namely that of God's restorative justice for the whole creation.*"[10] Jews saw the coming of the day of salvation as the coming of a new age, a new chapter of human history. The salvation life they expected to

---

[10] Wright, 165

live was the life of this coming age, which is the life of the age to come or what we popularly know as "eternal life."

The theology of a Pharisee can be summed up in three categories:

1. monotheism
2. election
3. eschatology

Jewish monotheism was the worship of Yahweh, the one true and living God who is the creator of all, yet distinct from his creation. The one God of Israel is the God who revealed himself to Abraham, Moses, and the prophets. Monotheism for the Pharisees was related to both covenant and creation. This God is the one who made a covenant with Abraham and this God is also the creator God who made everything that is. Election for Israel was their central belief that they were chosen by God to live in covenant with him as a part of his plan to rescue and redeem the whole world. Jewish eschatology was a look at the end of this age, specifically God's future for God's world including his actions in making the world right. These three themes in the context of Paul's Jewish world can be summed up in a single statement: Yahweh, the God of Israel had chosen Israel to be the people through whom God would use to fill the whole world with his glory.[11]

Athene and Her Owl: The Greek World

Paul did not develop his theology from the pagan world, but this fact does not mean he did not pick up nuggets of truth and wisdom from the culture around him. According to Wright, Paul believed,

---

[11] See Psalm 72:18; Numbers 14:20-23; Habakkuk 2:13; and Isaiah 11:9

"All wisdom of the world belongs to Jesus the Messiah in the first place, so any flickers or glimmers of light, anywhere in the world, are to be used and indeed celebrated within the exposition of the gospel."[12] The owl in Greek culture came to represent seeing, which serves as a fitting metaphor for Greek culture. The Greek philosophical tradition was built upon seeing what others could not see.

From a Greek point of view, Paul was doing three things which would be perceived more as philosophy than religion. First, Paul presented a different order of reality beginning with a creator God who had broken into creation. Greek philosophy, especially the philosophy of Plato, emphasized the importance of enlightenment in order to see reality as it was in actuality. Second, Paul taught and modeled a particular way of life quite different than the way of life known by the Greeks. Philosophy for the Greeks was not merely intellectual speculation detached from real life, but a way of living life. Third, Paul established and maintained communities resembling the many philosophical schools of the ancient world. Each branch of Greek philosophy had a gathering of people who came together to learn and grow with one another, not unlike the churches Paul planted.

Wright describes four primary school of Greek philosophy active in Paul's Greek world: the Academy, the Lyceum, the Stoics, and the Epicureans. The Academy was formed around the teachings of Plato, who taught the world of space, time, and matter were an illusion and less real than the world of "forms" or "ideas," which was ultimate reality. The Lyceum was built around Aristotle who taught the material world should be analyzed and categorized in the pursuit of virtue and *eudaimonia*, a Greek word best translated "human flourishing." The Stoics were a philosophical movement

---

[12] Wright, 201

that taught all material things were indwelt with divinity. The goal of the Stoic was to become a sage, to be wise, self-sufficient, and in harmony with the way things are. The Epicureans were a similar philosophical movement, but they taught that the gods were far removed and human beings have no eternal soul. The goal for Epicureans was to pursue tranquility and happiness in this life. In light of these Greek schools of thought Wright adds: "*Whereas the default mode of most modern westerners is some kind of Epicureanism, the default mode for many of Paul's hearers was some kind of Stoicism.*"[13] Epicureans were dualists. They believed in a sharp divide between the world of human beings and the world of the gods. Stoics were pantheists. They believed everything contained divine presence. Paul's Greek world was dominated by stoic thought.

Greek Stories and Questions

The Greeks were well known for their stories. Greek mythology was not a matter of entertainment, but a way of understanding the world. For example, the Platonists told creation stories. The "Allegory of the Cave" from Plato's *Republic* became a founding myth for the Greeks. This allegory tells the story of men bound in chains facing the back wall of a deep dark cave. They watch shadowy figures on the back of the wall and are unable to turn their heads. One man breaks free from his chains and turns around to see a bright fire with people waving puppets in front of the fire that casts shadows on the back wall. Further in the distance behind the fire, the freed man sees a glimmer of light. He makes the difficult ascent up the narrow passageway towards the mouth of the cave. When he reaches the

---

[13] Wright, 213

opening of the cave, his eyes are nearly blinded by the brightness of the sun. He struggles to see, but is able to see the reflections of trees and a mountain in a nearby lake. Eventually he is able to see clearly and he sees the world as it is in vivid color. This allegory served as a way for Platonists to describe the process of enlightenment where they could escape the illusionary physical world and see the world of perfect forms. Stoics told stories of creation by the *logos* or *pneuma* working with the primary elements: fire, air, earth and water. These stories fit neatly with the big questions in Greek culture: What is there? (questions about physics); what ought we do? (questions about ethics); and how do we know? (questions about logic).

A Rooster for Asclepius: Pagan Religion

Philosophy and religion overlapped in the pagan world surrounding Paul. The philosophers often spoke of the gods and there were quite a number of different religions being practiced in the ancient world. Paul's pattern of religion was fundamentally different than those around him even though it shared some similarities. His proclamation of a crucified Messiah was "a stumbling block to the Jews and foolishness to the Greeks."[14] For the Jews, a crucified Messiah was a failed Messiah and for the Greeks, the notion of one god was laughable. Religion, like Greek philosophy, was not separated from public life. The modern Western world has a clear dividing line between civic life and religious life. Sometimes these two lives are intertwined, but they still have distinguishable differences. Pagan religion in the Gentile world of Paul was woven into the very fabric of society. Pagan religions had temples, sacrifices, festivals, much like their Jewish counterpart and religion was a matter of action

---

[14] 1 Corinthians 1:23

more than stagnant belief. It was something a person did more than what a person believed. Religion bound together groups of people through the practice of certain rituals. Paul's preaching challenged pagan people with a new and different life made possible by Jesus the crucified and risen Jewish Messiah.

The Eagle has Landed: The Roman Empire

Rome took the eagle as its symbol for its power, beauty, and prestige. Rome in the day of Paul was ruled by the Caesar who installed local governors to oversee law and order throughout the empire. Caesar ruled the land promised to Messiah. According to Wright, "*After sixty years (of Roman civil war), they were ready for (peace). Ready, too, to make it divine, and to associate it with the man who had brought it: Pax Augusta. It was this 'peace' that allowed the apostle Paul, under Augustus's successors, to travel the world announcing a different peace, and a different master.*"[15] The Roman Emperor became the central symbol of Roman power and might.

The following Emperors ruled over one hundred years during the time of Jesus and Paul:

27 BC-14 AD	Augustus (Adopted son of Julius Caesar)
14-37 AD	Tiberius (Ruled during the life of Christ)
37-41 AD	Caligula
41-54 AD	Claudius (Ruled during the early ministry of Paul)
54-68 AD	Nero (Ruled during the later ministry of Paul)
68-69 AD	Galba (Ruled for 7 months)
69 AD	Otho (Ruled for 3 months)
69 AD	Vitellius (Ruled for 8 months)

[15] Wright, 288-289

69-79 AD	Vespasian (Ruled during the fall of Jerusalem)
79-81 AD	Titus (Son of Vespasian; the general in the siege of Jerusalem)
81-96 AD	Domitian (The beast from the bottomless pit in Revelation)

The fall of the Roman republic led to the Pax Romana under the Caesar, the Roman emperor. The Roman Empire used every cultural tool—from literature to coinage, from art to architecture—to promote the prestige and presence of Caesar. A sculpted bust of the emperor could be found everywhere, especially in major Roman cities, giving Roman citizens the impression that Caesar could see all. The growing popularity of Caesar led to the development of imperial cults, the worship of the emperor as a god. There was no one single unified cult, but many different imperial cults existed throughout the Roman Empire. The imperial cult was not a religion in the modern sense, but an interwoven part of life in the empire where religion, culture, and politics were interconnected.

The Roman Senate voted to divinize Augustus, giving him the title *divi filius*, meaning "son of god" or "son of the deified one." Augustus did not want public worship. His title was more of a way to honor him than an attempt to describe some kind of transformation of Augustus from a human being to a literal god. The announcement of Augustus' rise to power was called the "good news" bringing salvation to Rome. The worship of the emperor started small and began to grow. Tiberius was called son of god, son of the divine Augustus. Titus demanded to be called "lord and god." According to Wright, by the rule of Titus, "*Worshipping the emperors was well on the way to becoming a central and vital aspect not only of life in general but of civic and municipal identity. Whatever we say about either the intentions or the effects of Roman rulers from Julius Caesar to Vespasian, the richly diverse phenomena we loosely call 'imperial cult' were a vital part of a complex system of power, communication, and control, in other words, of all the things empires find they need to do."*[16]

Due in part to their understanding of God's future for his world, Jews had a fundamental objection to the Roman Empire. Wright notes, *"Rome's claim to have brought the world into a new age of justice and peace, flew, on eagle's wings, in the face of the ancient Jewish belief that these things would finally be brought to birth through the establishment of a new kingdom, the one spoken of in the Psalms, in Isaiah, in Daniel. Thus, though their resistance to empire drew on the ancient critique of idolatry, the sense that Israel's god would overthrow the pagan rule and establish his own proper kingdom in its place led the Jewish people to articulate their resistance in terms of eschatology."*[17] Jewish people were living under the rule of the empire, but they were not at all comfortable with it. They held tightly to the hope for the Messiah to come at long last and conquer the empire.

[16] Wright, 341
[17] Wright, 343

CHAPTER 3

PAUL'S WORLDVIEW

Paul and the Faithfulness of God, Chapters 6-8

As we move from history to worldview, Wright asks, *"So what happens when the owl, the (rooster) and the eagle are met by the bird that hovers over Israel?"*[1] In other words, what would it look like for philosophy, pagan culture and religion, and the politics of empire to coalesce into a multi-layered Gentile stream and collide with Paul's Jewish world? As a follower of Jesus the Messiah, Paul remained a Jewish thinker whose worldview was shaped by Greek philosophy, pagan religion, and Roman politics. These three other worlds offered symbols that were the mental furniture decorating Paul's primarily Jewish worldview. Reconstructing Paul's worldview is a necessary first step to understanding Paul's theology. As we have seen, Wright evaluates worldview based on four criteria: praxis, symbol, story, and question. He joins together praxis (practices) and

[1] Wright, 351

symbols in a singular phenomenon calling it "symbolic praxis" or symbols-in-action. In determining worldview based on core practices as symbols, Wright provides a thick description of Paul and his mindset.

Symbols in Paul's Mind

While we find many symbols in Paul's Jewish world, Wright chooses seven key symbols-in-action to begin to piece together Paul's worldview: Temple, Torah, prayer, land, family, zeal, and scripture. Each of these symbols were reworked in Paul's mind in light of Jesus the Messiah and the coming of the Holy Spirit. The Jewish temple was the dwelling place of Israel's God upon the earth, redefined by Paul as Jesus in his incarnation and, by the gift of the Holy Spirit, the church as the body of Messiah on earth. The Jewish Torah was the collected instructions for God's people to live as a worshipping and just community. It is helpful to think of the Torah in terms of symbols-in-action more than a list of rules. At the level of worldview, these symbols indicated what it looked like to be the people of God. Food and table fellowship had become a dominate symbol. Circumcision was a primary symbol. Keeping Sabbath was another important symbol. Jewish prayer was connected to both the Temple and the practice of turning one's self to the one true living God, the creator God. The *Shema* was central to Jewish prayer. Jewish land was the land promised to Abraham who was told that through him all the families of the earth will be blessed. This promise included land whereby Abraham and his descendants, "would be heir of the world."[2]

---

[2] Romans 4:13

The creator God's rule on the earth was not a "spiritual" rule, but an earthly, global one. According to Wright: "For Paul, God's kingdom — as we see clearly enough in 1 Corinthians 15:20-28 — is not a non-material, postmortem destination, but is rather the sovereign rule of the creator over the entire created order, with death itself, that which corrupts and defaces the good creation, as the last enemy to be destroyed. In other words, the final 'kingdom of God' is the whole world, rescued at least from corruption and decay, and living under the sovereign rule of God, exercised through the Messiah's people."[3] According to the story of Israel from the creation to the covenant with Abraham to the promises made to King David to the Jewish prophets, the God of Israel intended on restoring and reigning over the whole world and not merely one strip of land east of the Mediterranean Sea.

Jewish family was a picture of the people of God, reimagined as the community of the baptized by faith in Messiah. This symbol was not so much a picture of the traditional family in a Jewish context, but the entirety of Jewish people as the family of God. Jewish zeal was the willingness to take up arms to establish worship and justice, redefined by the reign of Jesus the Messiah as a battle against sin and death. Finally, Jewish scripture was the sacred text of the people of God, the story of Israel, a story in search of an ending, an ending ultimately found in Jesus the Messiah.

How did pagan symbols play out in Paul's mind? First and foremost, Paul would have recoiled at the sight of so many gods. According to Wright, Paul would have considered them to be "*man-made monstrosities.*"[4] As a conscientious Jewish thinker following Jesus the Messiah, Paul rejected the folly of idolatry, but Greek

[3] Wright, 367
[4] Wright, 375

philosophy, in Paul's mind, was something he would have considered helpful. Paul did not endorse a rejection of intellectual pursuits. On one occasion, Wright makes the claim that "Paul ranks with (Plato and Aristotle) as a thinker" as Paul wrestles with big ideas and conversations and synthesizes them in a new way.[5]

Roman festivals, which were common symbols-in-action in Paul's world, would have been less offensive than pagan worship. In his mind, Paul would have seen the duty in honoring, but not worshiping, those holding a position of civic authority. The honor Paul would have imagined was a quiet kind of honor without much attention given to it. Jesus was Lord after all and his kingdom had come. Paul would have been in favor of working for the good of the people within the empire, but would be quick to subvert the arrogance of the empire with unending devotion to Jesus. According to Wright, "*Paul did affirm the goodness, the God-givenness, of human structures of authority, even while at the same time undermining, through central aspects of his theology, the hubris, idolatry, blasphemy and other wickednesses which, as a Jew never mind as a follower of Jesus, he associated with the arrogance and swagger of Rome.*"[6] Many of the phrases used to exalt the emperor: "son of god," "lord of the world," "savior," "bringer of peace," and the rule which is "good news," Paul used to describe Jesus the Messiah.

---

[5] Wright makes this statement in an interview with Michael Bird, published by SPCK Publishing on September 9, 2012. http://youtu.be/sDHs8S1Se3E (Last accessed November 20, 2014)

[6] Wright, 381

Paul's Reconstructed Symbols-in-Action

Wright critiques established Protestant approaches to Paul's theology that have screened out what he considers to be the primary symbol-in-action in Paul's mindset: the community of the baptized, the church. Wright argues that Paul's letters, filled with his theological perspective, were not practices in self-understanding or detached philosophical investigation into the nature of God. Paul's letters were instructions for the lived-out practice of small communities of baptized followers of Jesus the Messiah spread out through the Mediterranean world of the Roman Empire. He tends to refer to the church as the *"ekklesia,"* the Greek word meaning public gathering or assembly. He uses this word for the church to avoid importing modern images of the local church and church structures into Paul's intended meaning of the word.

The fledgling, yet holy and unified, church was at the heart of Paul's worldview. Wright observes, *"The ekklesia and especially its unity stand at the centre of Paul's newly framed symbolic universe."*[7] The unity of the church as the one body of Messiah is the single thread binding together all of the writings of Paul. He did not write any clearer in this regard than in Galatians, where he writes, "There is neither Jew nor Greek, there is neither slave nor free, there is no male and female, for you are all one in Christ Jesus."[8] This symbol of unity was not an invention of Paul. Rather it grew out of an essentially Jewish vision. God's intention in his promise to Abraham was to have a single family who would worship the God of Israel and love one another justly. Yahweh, the God of Israel, was one—a powerful Jewish symbol of oneness reflecting God's nature and his desire for his people and indeed for all humanity to be one. For

---

[7] Wright, 387

[8] Galatians 3:28

Wright: "*The central symbol of Paul's newly formed world, the ekklesia, the Messiah's body, is nothing short of a new version of the human race.*"[9]

The people of God were not Jewish people and Gentile people but Messiah-people, Christ-people, which is to say: Christians. Jewish markers of identity had to be taken down and reworked in Paul's mind for the people of Messiah to be one as the God of Israel is one. Wright prefers to use the word "Messiah" instead of "Christ," so readers do not lose the sight of the Jewishness of Jesus' vocation. Jesus, in Wright's words, came as the "*strange and unexpected fulfillment of the story of Israel.*"[10] Messiah was the central focus of the unity of God's people and faith in Messiah functioned, at one level as a symbol. Messiah's people wore the badge of faith as a sign of membership in the covenant people of God.

The gospel in Paul's worldview contained three primary symbols: cross, resurrection, and lordship. The Messiah died on a cross for the sins of the world, including his own people, and provided the people of God a way to live in the world as a distinct people. He was crucified, subverting both the Jewish expectation of a zealous, violent King and the Roman authorities who used the cross to punish enemies. The cross symbolized the way to proclaim the kingdom through suffering and not conquest. The triumph over sin and death was put on display by the resurrection where the Messiah was vindicated and made Lord and King. The lordship of Jesus the Messiah stood as a subversive symbol for Jews and Gentiles, calling them to abandon their traditions and imperial loyalties to become the new, holy, and distinct people of the Messiah.

---

[9] Wright, 396
[10] Wright, 405

Followers of Jesus the Messiah, both Jews and Gentiles, did so as an act of worshipping the one God of Abraham, Isaac, and Jacob as seen in their prayers, reading of scripture, and the practice of communion. Baptism as a symbol of initiation into the body of Messiah represented a new exodus for the people of God, a rite of passage into the Messiah-family. According to Wright: *"The primary point of baptism, then, is not so much 'that it does something to the individual', it does, but that it defines the community of the baptized as the Messiah's people."*[11] Love in this baptized community was not an emotion but a practice and thus symbol-in-action, celebrated in the Eucharist and lived out in the partnership of the lives of the family of God. It was not a disembodied love, but a love centered in Jesus. The Messiah, for Wright, "is both the model and the means of love."[12] Paul imagined those in the Messiah would be a demonstration to the entire world of what God-designed humanity was to look like.

All humanity bears the image of Adam under sin. The newly-formed one people of God were to bear the image of God, which included a certain lifestyle inherited from the Jewish people. Some elements of Jewish life and worship were left behind, becoming irrelevant now that Messiah had come. Other aspects of Jewish life and ethics became intensified by the coming of Jesus the Messiah. Paul never saw Jewish practices as a list of rules, moral codes and principles, but as specific kinds of conduct lived in community. The appearing, and eventual vindication, of Jesus the Messiah marked the breaking in of the kingdom of God making available the life of the age to come. Wright refers to this as "inaugurated eschatology." The breaking in of the kingdom of God has been inaugurated, or

---

[11] Wright, 426

[12] Wright, 431

made official, in and through Jesus the Messiah. What God has made official is eschatology, that is, God's future for the world. The future life God desires has begun, but is not complete, in Jesus the Messiah and in the body of the Messiah, that is, the church. The community of faith lives the life of the age to come, and according to Wright: "*The community is supposed to live in reality how all humanity is supposed to live in theory.*"[13] As followers of Jesus the Messiah, we exemplify the life of the age to come, living and loving the way God designed.

These symbols-in-action are mental navigation points in Paul's worldview, shaping how he sees God, God's actions, God's people, God's world, and God's future. These symbols shape how Paul does theology as seen in his letters to the churches. Paul was not a detached observer of these things; he was personally involved as a pastor. He was not a Stoic believing everything was god, or an Epicurean, believing the gods were far away and unconcerned. He was a worshipper of the one God of Israel, the creator God. He was a follower of Jesus the Messiah and he was an active member of the Messiah-family.

Stories in Paul's Head

Paul's worldview contained not only moving symbols, but a story, a framing narrative that put the symbols together in an organized and coherent way. The story of Jesus the Messiah shaped Paul's worldview as it was not the story of Jesus as a timeless sage teaching universal truths, or Jesus as a rogue revolutionary starting a new religion, but Jesus as the Jewish Messiah. Jesus burst upon the scene in a specific socio-political context. He came as the long awaited

[13] Wright, 447

conclusion to the story of Israel. This story provided order to all the symbols in Paul's mind. We cannot make clear sense of the meaning of all of the symbols-in-action without a story. The "old perspective" on Paul tended to reject or minimize the story of Israel in Paul's theology. The "new perspective" on Paul tends to elevate the story of Israel in Paul's worldview and theology.

The framing narrative for the Jewish story is the larger story of the creator God and his creation. According to Wright, *"The creator God made a world with a purpose, and entrusted that purpose to humans... (and we are) presented with the fact that things are wrong, and that the creator needs to put them right."*[14] Creation and the subsequent world gone wrong comprise the essence of Genesis 1-11. Genesis 12, with the call of Abram, marks the beginning of the creator making things right. One of the common Jewish ways for speaking of the problem with creation and God's intention on setting things right was to speak of the "present age" and the "age to come."[15] The present age is the age of sin, evil, and death. The age to come, or eternal life to use a phase from the gospels, is the age of justice, peace, and life. These two ages overlap. The age to come has broken into the present age, but the present evil age continues to linger. The overlap of these ages reveals God's design not to scrap his good creation and toss it in the cosmic garbage can, but as Wright puts it: *"The creator intends to create a new world, a new kosmos, out of the womb of the old."*[16] Creation longs for this recreation as Paul describes it in Romans 8:18-25. God does not intend on abandoning his creation, but will be faithful to his

---

[14] Wright, 476

[15] For specific examples of this language in Paul see Romans 8:34-39; 1 Corinthians 2:1-10, 15:20-28; Colossians 2:14; and Ephesians 6:10-20

[16] Wright, 478

original plan. God's faithfulness to his creation (and later to his covenant with Israel) can be described as God's righteousness. Setting things right in a world gone wrong includes judgment, which *"is what restores health to a society, a balance to the world. It replaces chaos with order."*[17] God's righteousness, that is his faithfulness to creation, reveals his restorative justice.[18]

Subplots in Paul's Storied Worldview

Within the bigger story of God and creation, we find all sorts of subplots which, while smaller stories, are important in Paul's worldview. These subplots begin with God's special creation— humanity. As human beings we were created to bear God's image and care for God's world, but we have failed. We have become part of the problem; we need to be set right. God rescues us individually, not only for our individual benefit, but for the sake of our created vocation. God cannot set the world right without humanity rightly reflecting his image and rightly tending to his world. God offers salvation not merely for human beings to have a right relationship with him, language Paul never used, but for human beings to once again reflect the image of God into the world.

God chose Israel not merely to be in right relationship with him, but to reclaim humanity's original vocation to bear his image and tend to his world. The story of Israel is another subplot in the bigger story of creation. God's choosing and election of Israel was a matter of vocation not necessarily salvation. God has one single plan to save the world and it began with Abraham and ends with Jesus, the long-awaited Messiah. According to Wright, *"Paul*

---

[17] Wright, 481

[18] See Isaiah 11:1-10

reaffirms God's vocation to Israel, the vocation to be the means of rescuing humanity and thus creation itself, even though he radically redefines that vocation around the Messiah."[19] Israel failed in their vocation. They suffered in exile, waiting for Messiah, but God did not abandon them. Messiah comes while they continued to suffer, to liberate them so they could assume their vocation once again under the rule of Messiah.

The Torah, the Jewish law, played different roles in the story of Israel according to Paul. He calls the Torah good and holy in that it sets out to form Israel into the covenant people of God. Nevertheless, it also plays the role of a temporary guardian and is unable to produce the life of the age to come.[20] The sinful tendency[21] of humanity, including Israel, frustrates the purpose of Torah, causing it to play the role of agitator. Torah is not the bad guy in the story, but it plays the role of the instigator, arousing sinful desire.[22]

The story of Israel reached its conclusion in the story of Jesus. He came as Israel's promised Messiah, the seed of Abraham bringing the fulfillment of ancient promises. He came as the prophet like Moses leading Israel out of exile, and the Son of David restoring the kingdom to Israel. Jesus was Israel-in-person fulfilling Israel's vocation. According to Wright, Jesus *"is Adam; he is Israel; he is the Messiah. Only when we understand all this does Paul's worldview, particularly its implicit complex narrative, make sense."*[23] Jesus does for Israel, and for the world, what Israel could not do. As Adam, he

---

[19] Wright, 501

[20] Romans 8:3

[21] Or "flesh," Greek word: *sarx*

[22] See Romans 7:5

[23] Wright, 521

was rescuing people from this present evil age of sin and death and inviting people to enter into the new age of righteousness and life. Jesus demonstrated God's love and faithfulness to Israel and the world by his death, burial, and resurrection.

In summing up Paul's worldview, Wright asks five questions and supplies Paul's responses. (1) *Who are we?* We are the one people, Jew and Gentile, of the one God; we are Messiah's people bearing the mark of faith; we are the church. (2) *Where are we?* We live in God's world where Jesus the Messiah has begun his reign. (3) *What's wrong?* Sin, death, idolatry, and injustice have marred God's good world. (4) *What's the solution?* Prayer, the Spirit, and resurrection are the way forward. (5) *What time is it?* We live in the overlap of ages; the kingdom has already come and the kingdom has yet to come. God's future is here and it is coming.

CHAPTER 4

GOD: MONOTHEISM RETHOUGHT

Paul and the Faithfulness of God, Chapters 9

Paul's worldview shaped his theology, that is, what he believed about God, God's people, and God's future. When we explore his theology we begin to see his worldview in vivid detail. These two are inseparable. In Wright's words, worldview and theology are connected *"in a chicken-and-egg sort of way, as opposed to a fish-and-chips sort of way."*[1] Which comes first worldview or theology? This question reveals the interdependence of these two. Worldview is dependent upon theology, particularly the symbols-in-action within theology as seen in the last chapter, just as theology is dependent and guided by worldview.

Paul's theology is built around three primary elements of Jewish theology: monotheism, election, and eschatology. Paul did not reject Jewish elements of life and thought. According to Wright, he

---

[1] Wright, 609

"*rethought, reworked and reimagined them around Jesus the Messiah on the one hand and the Spirit on the other.*"[2] Jewish monotheism was the worship of Yahweh, the God of Israel, the creator God rethought in Paul's mind by Jesus and the Spirit. Jewish election was God's calling and vocation for Israel to be the one people of the one God rethought in light of Jesus' work to build his church through the Spirit. Jewish eschatology was God's future for God's world reimagined through the coming of Jesus the Messiah and the outpouring of the Spirit of Messiah. Paul taught and wrote as a Jewish thinker using Jewish language and concepts, which he radically reworked creating what we now know as Christian theology. This massive project begins with redefining what it means for God to be one.

Paul's Reaffirmation of Monotheism

Jewish monotheism in Paul's day was connected to Jewish kingdom theology, which was their robust belief in the kingdom of God. They believed the one God of Israel would come to rescue Israel and demonstrate his sovereign rule over the nations. The oneness of God was not so much a reference to the inner nature of God, but to God's supremacy over all other gods and rulers. The people of Israel swallowed up by the Roman Empire found themselves in the overwhelming minority as a people with only one god. Common sense in the ancient world said there were many, many gods. Whether the gods were present in the current order of things or not was a matter of debate, but there was no debating of the multiplicity of gods. The worshippers of the one God of Israel defended their claim based on the hope that their God would come

[2] Wright, 612

and deliver them from captivity, demonstrating his supremacy over all the pagan gods.

As the Roman Empire saw the rise in the worship of the emperor, and thus the worship of the empire, Jewish monotheism was viewed as a political threat. *"Empires thrive on religious relativism," according to Wright, "the more gods the better, since the more there are the less likely they are to challenge the ruling ideology."*[3] Paul expressed the cry of monotheism in a pagan world in various places in his letters. Paul writes, "Is God the God of Jews only? Is he not the God of Gentiles also? Yes, of Gentiles also, God is one—(and he) will justify the circumcised by faith and the uncircumcised through faith."[4] If we take the Jewish Shema—Hear, O Israel: The Lord our God, the Lord is one. You shall love the Lord your God with all your heart and with all your soul and with all your might—as the cornerstone of Jewish monotheism, we hear echoes of it in places like Romans 8:28: "to those who love God...." Paul further affirms monotheism in his reference to God as the creator and judge of the world. Jewish monotheism is best expressed not in speculative thoughts about the nature of God, but in the actions of God in history.[5]

Monotheism Rethought in Light of Jesus

Some scholars have speculated early Christians, including those of the apostolic era of Paul, did not believe Jesus of Nazareth was God in human form because this belief was not a Jewish idea. Wright

[3] Wright, 634

[4] Romans 3:29-30

[5] Paul frequently sites creation and judgment as examples of God's action in history, see Romans 1:19; 11:33-36; 1 Corinthians 15:23-28.

argues Paul, as well as the early Christians, did indeed believe Jesus was God due to the Jewish expectation of the return of Yahweh who would reign as king and rescue Israel from exile. Early Christians believe the God of Israel had returned in the person of Jesus and according to Wright: *"Jesus' first followers found themselves not only (as it were) permitted to use God-language for Jesus, but compelled to use Jesus-language for the One God."*[6]

We can find many examples of Paul redefining monotheism around Jesus the Messiah in his letters.[7] One clear example is in 1 Corinthians: "Therefore, as to the eating of food offered to idols, we know that 'an idol has no real existence,' and that 'there is no God but one.' For although there may be so-called gods in heaven or on earth—as indeed there are many 'gods' and many 'lords'—yet for us there is one God, the Father, from whom are all things and for whom we exist, and one Lord, Jesus Christ, through whom are all things and through whom we exist."[8]

The context surrounding these verses is the issue of eating food used as a sacrificial offering in pagan idol worship. Paul offers his pastoral guidance grounded in sound theology based in the *Shema*, where he writes "there is no God but one."[9] For Wright: *"To pray the Shema was to embrace the yoke of God's kingdom, to commit oneself to God's purposes on earth as in heaven, whatever it might cost. It was to invoke, and declare one's loyalty to the One God who had revealed himself in action at the Exodus and was now giving his people their*

---

[6] Wright, 655

[7] Wright chooses five texts in total as examples of monotheism rethought in light of Jesus: Galatians 4:1-11; Romans 8:1-4; 1 Corinthians 8:4-6; Colossians 1; 2 Corinthians 4:3-6; Philippians 2:6-11.

[8] 1 Corinthians 8:4-6

[9] 1 Corinthians 8:4

inheritance."[10] Followers of Jesus the Messiah worshiped the one God in a world with many gods, but for the Messiah's people "there is one God, the Father." Everything Paul has written so far is in line with Jewish thinking, but then he adds "...and one Lord, Jesus Christ." Compare the two lines from 1 Corinthians 8:6:

> one God, the Father, from whom are all things
> and for whom we exist

> one Lord, Jesus Christ, through whom are all things
> and through whom we exist

Paul has intentionally, and surprisingly for a Jewish audience, expanded the *Shema* to include Jesus in the way he describes the oneness of God. He described Jesus in the same words he uses in his description of God the Father. He added no explanation or argument, so we can assume a theological revolution had taken place among the primarily Jewish followers of Jesus the Messiah. According to Wright, "*Israel's God has returned at last in and as Jesus, (this) anchors the key worldview-symbol, the single community of the Messiah's followers. The revised Shema sustains both the unity and the holiness of the community.*"[11] Not only has the one God returned in and as Jesus the Messiah, but the Messiah has been crucified, increasing the redefinition of monotheism in shocking terms. For Wright, "*Paul sees the community of those who live by the rule of the One God, One Lord — which is the community of the crucified Messiah, defined by him in his death and resurrection — as the community in and through whom God's sovereign rule is coming to*

---

[10] Wright, 663

[11] Wright, 666

birth. To pray the revised Shema, just as much as the ancient one, was to take upon oneself the yoke of the kingdom."[12] The coming kingdom meant God had returned to his people, which Paul proclaims has happened in the coming of Jesus. He describes Jesus using categories belonging to Yahweh who had returned to his people.

Indeed, Jesus embodied the return of the one God of Israel in life, death, and resurrection. His resurrection on the third day revealed Jesus was indeed the Messiah. Paul writes: "(He) was declared to be the Son of God in power according to the Spirit of holiness by his resurrection from the dead, Jesus Christ our Lord."[13] As we have discovered, the Roman Empire used the title "Son of God" to speak of the Caesar, but for Jewish listeners the term spoke of the one sent from God. Jesus himself had called God his Father, so it seemed fitting to refer to Jesus as the Son. The resurrection did not create something new, but revealed what was already there, namely God is one but God is not singular.

In using the title "Lord" in reference to Jesus, Paul is implying that Yahweh himself is *"arriving in the person of the Messiah, at the climax of the story of Israel,"* because Jesus was doing what the people expected Yahweh to do.[14] "Lord" in the Old Testament is a reference to Yahweh. The confession "Jesus is Lord" brings about salvation for both the Jew and the Greek because, in quoting from the Old Testament, Paul claims the "same Lord is Lord of all" and "all those who call on the name of the Lord shall be saved."[15]

---

[12] Wright, 668

[13] Romans 1:4

[14] Wright, 705

[15] Romans 10:13

Monotheism Rethought in Light of the Spirit

The coming of Jesus the Messiah caused Paul to redefine what it meant for the God of Israel to be one God, but Paul's redefinition was not complete as he considered the coming of Jesus alone. He was also confronted by the coming of the Holy Spirit who was an integral part of the life of the church. Wright explains: "*The spirit was not, for Paul and his contemporaries, a 'doctrine' or 'dogma' to be discussed, but the breath of life which put them in a position to discuss everything else — and more to the point, to worship, pray, love and work.*"[16] The church's full articulation of the divinity of the Spirit came about in the fourth century, hundreds of years after Paul. Nevertheless the church fathers used the language of first century biblical writers to work out their descriptions of the Holy Spirit. For example, Irenaeus, a second century church father, wrote: "For with Him were always present the Word and Wisdom, the Son and the Spirit, by whom and in whom, freely and spontaneously, he made all things. This is to whom also he speaks, saying, 'Let Us make man after our image and likeness.'"[17] Paul used similar language in his pastoral prayers in Ephesians 1 and 3. Paul prayed: "the God of our Lord Jesus Christ, the Father of glory, may give you a spirit of wisdom," using the language of Father, Jesus, and spirit as a connected act.[18] While Paul did not make clear statements about the full divinity of the Son and the Spirit, he chose language connecting the Son and Spirit with God the Father.

The Spirit, like Jesus, was doing the sorts of things a first century Jewish person would expect Yahweh to do. The Spirit dwelling in the

---

[16] Wright, 710

[17] Quoted by David Bercot, *A Dictionary of Early Christian Beliefs*, Peabody, MA: Hendrickson, 104

[18] Ephesians 1:16; See also Ephesians 3:14-17

temple of our bodies was a picture of the long-awaited return of Yahweh to the temple. Paul asked: "Do you not know that you are God's temple and that God's Spirit dwells in you?"[19] The Spirit played the role of the Shekinah presence of God dwelling on the earth in this verse. Yahweh has returned to Zion through Jesus and the Spirit as he promised.[20] According to Wright: "*The Spirit is the personal, powerful manifestation of the One God of Jewish monotheism, the God who, having given Torah, has at last enabled his people to fulfill it and so come into the blessings of covenant renewal….*"[21] The Spirit enables us to do what the *Shema* requires in a new covenant by creating a new exodus out of sin and death and into the family of life.[22] The new temple where the Spirit works out this new covenant and new exodus is the gathering of Messiah's people.

In identifying both Jesus and the Spirit as accomplishing the work of Yahweh, Paul has radically rethought and redefined monotheism using Jewish language, imagery, and intent. The oneness of God in Jewish monotheism points to the rule of God as creator over the pagan gods worshiped by so many others. The God of Israel has come to deliver his people as he promised, but he came in a way nobody expected; he came through Jesus and the Spirit. Paul redefines monotheism within this framework. Wright describes this as a new exodus: "*The kingdom has been inaugurated through the work of Jesus, who, both as the embodiment of Israel's God and as the single bearer of Israel's destiny, has defeated the old enemy, has accomplished the new Exodus, and is now, by his spirit, leading his people to their inheritance—not, of course, 'heaven', but the reclaiming*

---

[19] 1 Corinthians 3:16

[20] See Isaiah 52:6-8

[21] Wright, 719

[22] See Jeremiah 31:31-34

of all creation."[23] Jesus and the Spirit did the works of Yahweh. This surprising revelation causes Paul to rethink what it means for God to be one.

Monotheism and the Problem of Evil

Paul viewed the problem of evil through his redefined Jewish monotheism. Wright observes: "The stronger your monotheism, the sharper your problem of evil. That is inevitable: if there is one God, why are things in such a mess?"[24] The Old Testament and the New Testament do not provide a detailed answer to the question, "Why is there evil and suffering in the world?" However Paul works within the Jewish tradition of not providing answers to the "why" question, but offering responses regarding what the creator intends to do about evil in his world.

The problem of evil, that is the plight of Israel and humanity, has been rethought by Paul in light of Jesus and the gift of the Spirit, just as monotheism had been rethought. Paul understood the problem of idolatry and injustice contributing to evil and suffering in the world, and he found the solution to the problem in the death/resurrection of Jesus and the coming of the Spirit. The hideous and unthinkable crucifixion of the Messiah was, for Paul, God's answer to the problem. If the answer required the death of the Son of God, then the plight was far worse than Paul first imagined.

Paul's initial thoughts regarding the plight were simple: it was a problem with the pagan nations. However if the plight was essentially a problem with pagan/Gentile nations oppressing and preventing Israel from fulfilling her vocation to be a light of salvation to the world, then

[23] Wright, 735
[24] Wright, 737

why did the Jewish Messiah have to be crucified? The problem was not merely the Gentiles not acting like Jews or the oppression of Jews by the Roman Empire, although oppression itself was part of the problem. The deeper problem revealed in the death of the Messiah was sin and death itself. Israel, while the chosen covenant people of God, had become a part of the problem, too, as they were not immune to the sickness of sin. The Messiah was crucified so sin could be condemned and death could be defeated.[25] The plight is both personal and cosmic, both individual and corporate, both a Gentile problem and a Jewish problem.

The death and resurrection of the Messiah revealed the deeper issues within the plight of humanity, and the Spirit reveals these deeper issues, too. The Spirit came to do what the Torah alone was unable to do, to transform and renew the hearts of God's people. The transformational work of the Spirit would produce the life promised in God's covenant with Israel. According to Wright: "*The One God had revealed this 'life' both in the resurrection of Jesus, in the promise of resurrection for all Jesus' people, and in the new moral shaping of their present lives. This was what the Torah could not do, because by itself it could not in fact deal with either sin or death.*"[26] The problem revealed by sin and death was not only that individuals were guilty and subject to the judgment of God, but sin and death prevented the covenant community of God from carrying out God's purposes to save and restore the world.

Paul described the issue of judgment in Romans 1. The wrath of God has been revealed against unrighteous and ungodly men.[27] For Paul the "wrath of God" was a picture of the divine punishment

---

[25] See Romans 8:3

[26] Wright, 759

[27] Romans 1:18

of sinners. This is future judgment for those of whom Paul wrote "are storing up wrath for yourself on the day of wrath when God's righteous judgment will be revealed."[28] Gentiles are without excuse because they have seen God's attributes in creation. Jews who practice evil and yet judge the Gentiles are equally complicit in the plight. "There will be tribulation and distress for every human being who does evil, the Jew first and also the Greek, but glory and honor and peace for everyone who does good, the Jew first and also the Greek. For God shows no partiality."[29] The one God of Israel is the God of both the Jews and the Gentiles. He desires for them both to carry out his purposes on the earth, but for those who chose a course of destruction, who become the perpetrators of evil and suffering in the world, they will be dealt with in a final act of judgment by the one God.

[28] Romans 2:5

[29] Romans 2:9-11

CHAPTER 5

GOD'S PEOPLE: ELECTION REDEFINED

Paul and the Faithfulness of God, Chapters 10

For Wright, "election" in Paul's vocabulary refers to "choosing," but not in the modern sense of voting. Election-as-choosing for Paul was not what is reflected in certain doctrines of predestination whereby God has chosen some for salvation (the elect) and chosen others for damnation (the reprobate). According to Wright, "*The word 'election', as applied to Israel, usually carries a further connotation: not simply the divine choice of this people, but more specifically the divine choice of this people for a particular purpose.*"[1] In other words, election for Paul is about vocation not salvation.

As with monotheism, election was a Jewish concept he had rethought around Jesus the Messiah. Election includes salvation, the work of God rescuing, healing, and justifying. Justification is the act of God as judge in a court of law pronouncing "in the right" those

---

[1] Wright, 775

who are guilty, but from a Jewish point of view, it means something more. God justifies, puts people right, in order to carry out his purposes. Israel's purpose was to bear God's image and tend to God's world, a direct echo of Adam's purpose. Adam was given a garden; Israel was given land. Adam received commands; Israel received commands. Adam disobeyed and was exiled; Israel disobeyed and was exiled. The God of Israel came in the person of the Messiah and the Spirit to do what Adam and Israel could not do. In this sense, Jesus and the Spirit did not replace Israel, but fulfilled Israel's vocation.

Understanding how Paul used the term "election" requires an understanding of righteousness. Wright uses the word "covenant" in his definition of righteousness, thus revealing Abraham as the answer to Adam. God made a promise to bless and save the nations of the world through Abraham, a promise expressly seen in the exodus event. God's promise to Abraham was his response to the proliferation of sin and death brought on by Adam's disobedience. "Righteousness" in Paul's letters can mean:

1. right behavior: ...one act of righteousness leads to justification and life for all men.[2]
2. Legal, or covenant, status: Those who receive...the free gift of righteousness...[3]
3. moral character (in reference to people): For the kingdom of God is not a matter of eating and drinking but of righteousness and peace and joy in the Holy Spirit.[4]
4. covenant faithfulness (in reference to God): But now the

---

[2] Romans 5:18

[3] Romans 5:17

[4] Romans 14:17

righteousness of God has been manifested apart from the law...[5]

A better English word for the Greek word *dikaiosune*, most often translated "righteousness," is "just" or "justice." When Paul wrote about God's righteousness, he was writing about God's covenant faithfulness and/or his restorative justice. God's own righteousness is his faithfulness to his covenant to bless the world through the people of Abraham.[6]

Israel's Election

God's righteousness is connected to Israel's role as the instrument by which God would save the world. The God of Abraham, Isaac, and Jacob did not choose Israel so he could be "best friends" with one ethnic group. According to Wright, "*Yahweh's choice of Israel as his people, was aimed not simply at Israel itself, but at the wider and larger purposes which this God intended to fulfill through Israel. Israel is God's servant; and the point of having a servant is not that the servant becomes one's best friend, though that may happen too, but in order that, through the work of the servant, one may get things done.*"[7] Through Israel, the one God, the God of creation, the God of Israel intended to bring his righteous rule to the entire world. This promise has been fulfilled through Jesus the Messiah and the coming of the Spirit upon the body of Messiah, the church. Does this mean the people of Messiah have replaced the people of Abraham as the people of God? Did Paul teach a so-called

---

[5] Romans 3:21

[6] See Isaiah 9:7, 42:6

[7] Wright, 804

"replacement theology"? Wright answers with an emphatic "no." Jesus does not replace Israel. The church does not replace Israel. Jesus is after all Israel's Messiah. He does not replace Israel; he embodies Israel and fulfills Israel's vocation to be the agency whereby God would bless the world. This vocation was the purpose of election from the beginning. Yahweh did not choose Abraham, and thus Israel, in order to damn the rest of the world. Just the opposite is true. God chose Israel to bless the world. In fulfilling Israel's mission, Jesus redefines what it means to be Israel. Paul writes, "For no one is a Jew who is merely one outwardly, nor is circumcision outward and physical. But a Jew is one inwardly, and circumcision is a matter of the heart, by the Spirit, not by the letter. His praise is not from man but from God."[8]

Messiah was the location where the one God of Abraham and the one people of Abraham met. In other words, Messiah was where monotheism and election came together in beautiful harmony. When Paul proclaimed Jesus as Messiah, he was demonstrating how the entire purpose of Israel's election had found its intended termination point. Paul drew on royal passages from Psalms and Isaiah in speaking of Jesus who came as God's servant to confirm the promises of Israel so Gentiles could see God's mercy.[9] Messiah brought the conclusion to the law, bringing the long awaited ending to Israel's story. Paul used incorporative language in talking about Messiah. Jesus incorporates the identity and mission of Israel into himself. In other words, Jesus as Messiah incorporates both the defining markers of what it meant to be the people of God, and the calling the people of God were to obey, in order to become Israel in human form. Israel was God's servant, so Israel's Messiah was God's

---

[8] Romans 2:28-29
[9] See Romans 15:8-12; Psalm 18:49, 117:1; Isaiah 11:10

servant. What could be said of Israel could be said of Messiah. Jesus was Israel in the flesh.

Those who were "in Messiah" were therefore bearers of Israel's identity and mission. According to Wright: *"To be 'in the king,' or now, for Paul, 'in the anointed one,' the Messiah, is to be part of the people over which he rules, but also part of the people who are defined by him, by what has happened to him, by what the one God has promised him."*[10] To be in Christ, which is in the Messiah, is to be in "Israel" as the people of God. Israel in this sense is redefined, but not replaced. Paul's redefinition of election fulfills the new covenant spoken of by the Hebrew prophets. Paul writes, "Now the promises were made to Abraham and to his offspring. It does not say, 'And to offsprings,' referring to many, but referring to one, 'And to your offspring,' who is Christ."[11] The Messiah is the child of Abraham and those in the Messiah are also children of Abraham. Wright describes this incorporation as a new solidarity: *"Paul regarded Jesus as Israel's Messiah, and that he saw and expressed that belief in terms of Messiah's summing up of Israel in himself, thereby launching a new solidarity in which all those 'in him' would be characterized by his 'faithfulness', expressed in terms of his death and resurrection."*[12] For Wright, seeing the theme of faithfulness in God displayed in the Messiah, and in the people of God, becomes one of the keys to understanding Paul's theology.

Jesus the Faithful Messiah

Wright argues persuasively for a rereading of key passages in Romans and Galatians, particularly in how we understand what is

[10] Wright, 830

[11] Galatians 3:16

[12] Wright, 835

commonly translated "faith in Jesus Christ." In Romans 3 Paul writes, "The righteousness of God through faith in Jesus Christ for all who believe. For there is no distinction."[13]

The question is should we translate this "faith in Jesus Christ" or the "faithfulness of Jesus Christ?" The Greek phrase does not contain a preposition. The Greek word *pistis* can be translated "faith" or "faithfulness." Is Jesus the object or the subject of this Greek phrase? If Jesus is the object, then we should translate it "faith in Jesus;" he would be the object of our action. If Jesus is the subject of the phrase, then we should translate this phrase "faithfulness of Jesus," with faithfulness describing something of the character of Jesus. Wright argues for a reading of this verse with Jesus as the subject. He writes, "*The faithfulness which was required of Israel, but not provided, has now been provided by Israel's representative, the Messiah.*"[14] Part of the challenge of interpreting scripture includes wrestling to translate individual verses in a way that is faithful to the author's intent. Where the specific verse is not clear, the best solution is to look at the verse in context.

Wright backs up to Romans 2:24-29. This text sets the context for our interpretive question in Romans 3:22. The context is a question itself as we saw above: Who is a Jew? Paul answers: "No one is a Jew who is merely one outwardly, nor is circumcision outward and physical. But a Jew is one inwardly, and circumcision is a matter of the heart, by the Spirit, not by the letter. His praise is not from man but from God."[15] Paul radically redefines what it means to be a Jew, the chosen people of God. To be marked as a member of God's covenant family is not the marker of physical circumcision, but a circumcision of the heart.

[13] Romans 3:22

[14] Wright, 837

[15] Romans 2:28-29

Paul's thought process in Romans 2:24-29 continues into Romans 3. He asks, "Then what advantage has the Jew?"[16] Answer: "Jews were entrusted with the oracles of God."[17] Then Paul asks, "What if some were unfaithful (in their vocation)? Does their faithlessness nullify the faithfulness of God?"[18] The context here is the faithfulness of Israel contrasted with the faithfulness of God. Romans 3:9-20 makes it clear: Israel shares in the failure of humanity to reflect God's image. Israel, too, is under sin. Israel has not been faithful to the oracles of God entrusted to them. According to Wright, "*If the covenant God is going to bless the world through Israel, he needs a faithful Israelite.*"[19] With this context in mind, we can revisit Romans 3:22. Paul argues the righteousness of God has been manifested apart from the Jewish Law, even though the law points to it. Wright translates Romans 3:22: "God's covenant justice comes into operation through the faithfulness of Jesus the Messiah, for the benefit of all who have faith."[20]

Faith in Jesus, while essential, does not demonstrate God's righteousness, which is his covenant faithfulness and justice. Rather, the faithfulness of Jesus, namely his faithful death, displays the brightness and integrity of God's covenant faithfulness. Personal faith in Jesus is still necessary if a person is to experience justification, which is why Paul adds "for all who believe" after he writes of the faithfulness of Jesus.[21] Israel has been unfaithful.

---

[16] Romans 3:1

[17] Romans 3:2

[18] Romans 3:3

[19] Wright, 839

[20] Romans 3:22, *The Kingdom New Testament*

[21] Romans 3:22

Conversely, Jesus the Messiah as Israel-in-person has been faithful; he proudly wears the badge of faithfulness. Faith, and not the law, then becomes the badge worn by the Messiah-people who are identified as the people of God. In wearing the badge of faith, human beings, both Jews and Gentiles, are justified, that is, declared by God to be members of his covenant family.

The faithfulness of God has been demonstrated through the redemption that is in Jesus the Messiah. Redemption language in Romans 3 draws upon Jewish imagery, namely the celebrated Passover event when God rescued Israel from Egyptian slavery. God has passed over sin, but now sin has been finally and completely dealt with at the cross. Messiah's people are set right as members of the covenant people not by living out the Torah, but by living by faith, a faith in Jesus that sums up the intended purpose of the law.[22]

The issue in Paul's redefinition of election—those chosen to be the people of God who carry out the mission of God on the earth—is to make the point that God is the King of Gentiles as well as Jews.[23] The language used by Paul fits with both the interpretation of those who see Romans 2 and 3 as having to do with legal status before God and those who see these chapters as having to do with human participation. Paul expresses in Romans 3:38 that we are justified by faith apart from the law. According to Wright this statement implies we are "*reckoned to be within the justified people, those whom this God has declared 'righteous', 'forgiven', 'members of the covenant', on the basis of pistis (faith) alone.*"[24]

[22] See Romans 3:31

[23] Romans 3:29

[24] Wright, 847

Faithfulness and Justification

According to Paul in Galatians 2:16, a person is not justified by works of the law but through the faithfulness of Jesus Christ. Wright adds: *"Justification is all about being declared to be a member of God's people; and this people is defined in relation to the Messiah himself."*[25] When we are justified, we are declared to be in the right and thus members of God's covenant community. For Paul, the issue of being justified by works is not so much about individuals attempting to earn salvation by what they have done. Rather, the issue is with the Jewish people using their works as the primary marker of their membership in God's family. The Jews who rely on the works of the law as the badge of membership in the family of God are under a curse, but Jesus redeems Israel from the curse by becoming a curse for them.[26] Through the redemption of Jesus, God's promise to Abraham comes true so that the blessing of Abraham might come on the people of the entire world. Jesus' redeeming death demonstrates God's faithfulness to the covenant.

So what is the purpose for the Torah?[27] Paul's answer can be summed up in one word: sin. The Torah served as a stand-in, a babysitter, until Messiah came. According to Wright, *"Torah offered life, it could not give it—not through its own fault, but through the sinful human nature of the Israel to which it had been given."*[28] The law was necessary, but temporary. It initially created two families where the one God of Israel ultimately desired one people. For Wright, this desire connects election with monotheism: *"How do we know that this God desires that single family? Because God is*

[25] Wright, 856

[26] Galatians 3:13

[27] Galatians 3:19

[28] Wright, 871

one....Monotheism, freshly understood through Messiah and spirit, provides the ground and source for the fresh christological understanding of election."[29] The law was not wrong. It was not opposed to the promises of God, but because of human sinfulness, including the sins of Israel, it was set on a course to enslave God's people.

God has been faithful to his promises to bless the world through the people of Abraham. God acted in and through Jesus the Messiah. Messiah's people now have been invited to participate in what he has done. Paul describes this two-fold process in 2 Corinthians 5 where he celebrates the achievement of the Messiah and then describes the invitation to participate. Paul writes:

"He died for all (*Messiah's achievement*), that those who live might no longer live for themselves but for him who for their sake died and was raised (*the implementation and our participation*)."[30]

"God through Christ reconciled us to himself (*Messiah's action*) and gave us the ministry of reconciliation (*our participation*)..."[31]

"For our sake he made him to be sin who knew no sin (*Messiah's action*), so that in him we might become (embody) the righteousness of God *(our participation)*."[32]

The death of Messiah brought all sin—the plight of humanity—to a single point where it could be condemned and its power broken. Paul writes: "For God has done what the law,

---

[29] Wright, 872

[30] 2 Corinthians 5:15

[31] 2 Corinthians 5:18

[32] 2 Corinthians 5:21

weakened by the flesh, could not do. By sending his own Son in the likeness of sinful flesh and for sin, he condemned sin in the flesh, in order that the righteous requirement of the law might be fulfilled in us, who walk not according to the flesh but according to the Spirit."[33] Paul again uses the two-fold language of achievement and participation in describing the cross as the central point where salvation, and indeed justification, is made possible. God condemns sin in and through the Messiah's faithful death on the cross and we are invited to participate in the benefits of this action by walking according to the Spirit. In Wright's words: "*The cross is, for Paul, the sign of the centre: the centre for Israel, the centre for humankind. It is the middle of everywhere, the definite line which refocuses edge-lured minds, the axis of everything.*"[34] The cross where the Messiah displays the faithfulness of God has become a new axis for the entire world and also a new axis for Paul's theology.

The grand achievement of Jesus the Messiah including his faithful death on the cross, and the outpouring of the Spirit upon the church, caused Paul to rethink the meaning of the people of God. The gospel for Paul was the announcement that the God of Israel has been faithful to his covenant by fulfilling his promises through Jesus the Messiah and the coming of the Spirit. The gospel was not how to get saved from sin or how to be justified or how to have a personal relationship with God. The gospel was, and is, the royal announcement of what God has done in and through Jesus' death, burial, and resurrection. The gospel announcement comes with the work of the Spirit for no one can say "Jesus is the Lord" without the Spirit.[35] Furthermore, the Spirit accomplishes in the

---

[33] Romans 8:3-4

[34] Wright, 910

[35] 1 Corinthians 12:3

renewed people of God what the Torah could not do in the initial people of God. The people of God are no longer people of the Torah, but people of the Spirit.

The Shape of Justification

Paul discusses justification in the context of his reworking of the election of Israel summed up in Jesus the Messiah and lived out in the one people of God by the Holy Spirit. The logic of Israel's election was not God choosing one ethnic group in order to condemn the rest of the world or allow them to remain in pagan darkness. The logic of the election of Israel was God choosing a certain people through whom he would rescue the world with the light of his love. To be justified is to be put right as the people of God for the purposes of God. In order to see the logic of election within the overarching purposes of God, Wright sketches seven movements which capture the logical context behind his interpretation of Paul's theology of justification.

1. *"God the creator intends at the last to remake the creation, righting all wrongs and filling the world with his own presence."*[36] We begin where the Christian narrative begins; we start with the actions of the one true God making the world as a place to be shared with human beings.

2. *"For this to happen, humans themselves have to be 'put right'."*[37] Humanity is intricately connected to God's world, so they must be put right. God's way of putting people right is God's act of justification.

[36] Wright, 926
[37] Wright, 926

3. "*God's way of accomplishing this is through the covenant.*"[38] Even though it may seem like a strange way of setting things right, covenant was, and is, God's way of redeeming his good creation. God intended all along to remain faithful to Israel.

4. "*(The covenant) is how the creator God will put humans to rights.*"[39] God is responsible for setting right a world gone wrong and he has the power and authority to do so. He will not only set the world right through covenant, but his covenant with Israel was his particular way of setting all of humanity right.

5. "*All these themes point forward to the decisive divine judgment on the last day, in other words, to 'final eschatology.'*"[40] All language regarding justification points to God's future and final act of judgment, where he will sort out the things gone wrong in his good world. Present justification experienced by those in Jesus the Messiah is a foretaste of the justification to come at the final judgment.

6. "*The events concerning Jesus the Messiah are the revelation, in unique and decisive action, of the divine righteousness.*"[41] In the death of Jesus, sin—the source of humanity's wrongdoing—is condemned, and in the resurrection of Jesus, God's new creation, the very place where the world is being put right, has begun. Through the Messiah we see God's righteousness

[38] Wright, 927

[39] Wright, 934

[40] Wright, 936

[41] Wright, 942

displayed both in terms of his covenant faithfulness and his restorative justice.

7. *"When Paul speaks about people being 'justified' in the present, he is (arguing)...that in the present time the covenant God declares 'in the right,' 'within the covenant,' all those who hear, believe and obey 'the gospel' of Jesus the Messiah."* [42] This declaration creates a new situation, a new status for those who are justified and thus welcomed in as the people of God. Justification is not a description of a person's moral character but a declaration of a person's social identity. Wright adds: *"Those who are declared or accounted 'righteous' on the basis of Messiah-faith constitute the single covenant family which the one God has faithfully given to Abraham."*[43]

With the logical framework behind Paul's understanding of justification established, Wright turns his attention towards examining how Paul uses the concept of justification in five key passages.

Justification at Work in Galatians 2:15-4:11

Paul writes, "We ourselves are Jews by birth and not Gentile sinners; yet we know that a person is not justified by works of the law but through faith in Jesus Christ, so we also have believed in Christ Jesus, in order to be justified by faith in Christ and not by works of the law, because by works of the law no one will be justified."[44]

[42] Wright, 944
[43] Wright, 961
[44] Galatians 2:15-16

Just as with his translation of Romans 3:22, Wright translates "faith *in* Jesus" in Galatians 2:16 as "the faithfulness *of* Jesus." The context of this passage in Galatians was the so-called "Antioch incident" where Peter chose not to share a table with Gentile Christians. Paul confronted Peter because his sin was fundamentally a gospel-issue as he explains in Galatians 2:15. We are not justified—declared righteous and therefore members of God's people—because we keep the law, but because of the faithfulness of Jesus. We believe in Jesus and are justified, but as we have seen, our justification is based on Jesus' faithful death. Our faith is the badge indicating we are members of God's people. The primary reason Wright translates this phrase in Galatians 2 "faithfulness of Jesus" is the context: *"Paul's whole argument is about membership in the single family, sharing the same table-fellowship, not primarily about the way in which sins are dealt with and the sinner rescued from them."*[45] There is little mention of sin, and no mention of death, in Galatians. The letter focuses on the definition of Christian community, that is: What does it mean to be the people of God? What are the markers defining Christian community? This definition has been reworked around Jesus the Messiah and the coming of the Spirit. Paul writes, "Are you so foolish? Having begun by the Spirit, are you now being perfected by the flesh?"[46] Paul was addressing the Galatians (plural) according to 3:1. He was not asking whether or not individual Christians in Galatia were trying to carry on their private, personal relationships with God by the flesh. Paul's thoughts were on the community. These justified people, in response to the faithfulness of Jesus the Messiah, were becoming one people by the work of the Spirit.

---

[45] Wright, 969

[46] Galatians 3:3

This called people, the children of Abraham, redefined by Jesus and the Spirit will be the means by which God blesses the nations.[47] The promise given to Abraham was not merely for one ethnic people (the Jews) in one particular land (Israel); the promise was for the whole world. Jesus became a curse for Israel, redeeming them from the curse of the law so that the blessing promised to Abraham may come to the Gentiles.[48] Jesus the Messiah became a curse for Israel so that "we (both Jews and Gentiles) might receive the promised Spirit through faith."[49] To be declared righteous members of God's chosen people (election) has been redefined. Members who once were marked by keeping the Torah are now marked by both faith in Jesus as Messiah whose faithful death demonstrated God's faithfulness to the Torah and the reception of God's Spirit.

Justification at Work in 2 Corinthians 3:3

Paul writes, "And you show that you are a letter from Christ delivered by us, written not with ink but with the Spirit of the living God, not on tablets of stone but on tablets of human hearts."[50] The people of God have been redefined by and through the Holy Spirit who has come in fulfillment of Jeremiah's prophecy of a new covenant where the one God of Israel would write his laws

---

[47] Galatians 3:8

[48] Wright understands the "us" in Galatians 3:13 to be the Jewish people. He argues for this interpretation because the Gentiles are not under the law and are therefore not under the curse of the law. This interpretation seems to balance well with Paul's focus on the blessing coming upon the Gentiles.

[49] Galatians 3:14

[50] 2 Corinthians 3:3

on the hearts of his people.[51] The coming of a new covenant implies a new definition of election as the people of God. According to Wright, "*The spirit has redefined 'election', the covenant status of the people of God. The covenant is not now a matter of possessing or hating the Mosaic law. It is a matter of the transformation of the heart, wrought by the spirit.*"[52] The Shekinah glory of God which under the old covenant dwelt in a particular place, the Temple in Jerusalem, now dwells in the hearts of God's people.

Justification at Work in Philippians 3:2-11

Paul writes, "...and be found in him, not having a righteousness of my own that comes from the law, but that which comes through faith in Christ, the righteousness from God that depends on faith."[53] Paul describes receiving righteousness from God in the context of those who define covenant membership by circumcision and thus, adherence to the Torah. The statement "for we are the circumcision, who worship by the Spirit of God..."[54] refers to the redefined "we," redefined by the coming of the Spirit.

Paul continues by recounting his Jewish heritage. He was not bragging that he had earned points as a Jew and was somehow self-righteous. He was providing the evidence that he was a legitimate part of the covenant family, but none of that mattered to Paul after the Messiah had come. Paul describes his covenant status as in the Messiah. Wright translates Philippians 3:9 according to the idea of covenant status: "...that I may be discovered in him, not having my

---

[51] See Jeremiah 31:31-34

[52] Wright, 983

[53] Philippians 3:9

[54] Philippians 3:3

own covenant status (righteousness) defined by Torah, but the status (righteousness) which comes through the Messiah's faithfulness: the covenant status (righteousness) from God which is given to faith."[55] Paul is not claiming God has somehow imputed to him God's righteous nature or the moral character of Christ, rather God has conferred upon him a status whereby he knew he was in the covenant with God's covenant people. According to Wright, "*Being 'in the Messiah', as clearly here as anywhere in Paul, is the new way of saying 'in Israel.'*"[56] Justification is not a matter of the forgiveness of personal sin, but incorporation into the Messiah and into Messiah's people.

Justification at Work in Romans 3:21-4:25

This section is one complete thought, revealing the righteousness of God on display, not the righteousness we receive from God which Paul described in Philippians 3:9. In Romans 3, Paul indicates God's covenant faithfulness has been displayed apart from the law and through the faithfulness of Jesus for the benefit of those who believe. There is no distinction between Jews and Gentiles; both are given over to sin and subject to death. The good news is both are justified, declared to be members of God's family, by grace. Wright explains: "*What we loosely think of as 'justification' is very closely joined in Paul's mind with the incorporation of believers into the messianic reality of Jesus death and resurrection.*"[57] We are justified through the redemption that is in Jesus the Messiah. Paul describes the death of Jesus using sacrificial terms: "blood," "atoning sacrifice," and "passed

---

[55] Philippians 3:9, *The Kingdom New Testament*

[56] Wright, 989

[57] Wright, 997

over." God was demonstrating his faithfulness to the covenant to bless the world through Israel which included the practice of ritualistic sacrifice, but the Messiah's death meant the fulfillment and end of the sacrificial system. The redefined people of God, the church, would no longer carry on that practice. Wright sees the faithful death of Jesus as a death that ends sacrifice and exemplifies the faithfulness of God: "*The 'righteousness' of God which was called into question by the failure of Israel to be 'faithful' to the divine commission (3:2-3) has been put into effect through the faithfulness of Messiah.*"[58]

No one gets to boast, not Jews and not Gentiles, because both are justified according to the covenant faithfulness of God revealed in the faithful death of Jesus. God is the God of both Jews and Gentiles, because "God is one."[59] God is the one God of all peoples and he justifies all by faith. Wright explains: "*This new people is composed, not only of Gentiles, of course, but of Jews and Gentiles alike who display this pistis* [Greek word for "faith"], *the badge of membership. This is the same badge, whether one's covenant status is renewed or initiated.*"[60]

In Romans 4 Paul moves to a discussion of Abraham, not as an example of how individuals "get saved" by faith, but as continuation of the display of God's faithfulness to his covenant with Abraham. Paul asks, "What then shall we say was gained by Abraham, our forefather according to the flesh?"[61] He did not gain a personal relationship with God; he gained seminal membership into God's

---

[58] Wright, 1000

[59] Paul connects monotheism with election in Romans 3:30 with a direct echo of the *Shema*.

[60] Wright, 1001

[61] Romans 4:1

family. Abraham wore the badge of faith and God declared him to be a member of God's own family. Paul continues: "The purpose was to make him the father of all who believe without being circumcised, so that righteousness would be counted to them as well."[62] God did not choose Abraham in order to disregard the Gentile nations. God chose Abraham to extend access to the covenant to all those who believed in the Messiah. The covenant was all about God having one family of Jews and Gentiles.

What was God's promise to this one family? According to Paul, "the promise to Abraham and his offspring, that he would be heir of the world...."[63] The redefined people of God would be occupants of the whole world. God made a promise of land to Abraham, but the promised land has been redefined, as with everything else, around the coming of Messiah and the gift of the Spirit; the promised land is now the whole earth. This promise did not come through the Torah, rather it come through the display of God's covenant faithfulness through the faith of His people who share the faith of Abraham who was "fully convinced that God was able to do what he had promised."[64] Abraham wore the badge of faith and was included in God's family; we wear the badge of faith and we are included in God's family because Jesus died for our sins and was raised from the dead for our justification, our inclusion in God's family.

Justification at Work in Romans 5-8

Wright suggests we start somewhere in the middle of this section, where Paul writes: "We are released from the law, having died to

[62] Romans 4:11

[63] Romans 4:13

[64] Romans 4:21

that which held us captive, so that we serve in the new way of the Spirit and not in the old way of the written code."[65] This section continues with the theme of the covenant people of God redefined by Jesus and, particularly noted here, by the Spirit. The Holy Spirit was not anything other than the spirit of the God of Israel. According to Wright: "*The spirit is not some alien force, but rather the fresh (though long-promised) manifestation of the one God of Jewish monotheism.*"[66] In Romans 7, Paul was specifically addressing Jewish Christians because in telling the story of the redemption of Israel, he was telling the story of the redemption of the world. This section reverberates with themes of a new exodus, where sin is the slave master, baptism is the Red Sea crossing, and the redeemed world is the promise land.

According to Wright, Paul was not discussing his struggle with sin either pre- or post-conversion in Romans 7:15-25. Paul was not describing the normal Christian life as a life-long struggle with sin. When Paul wrote, "For I do not understand my own actions. For I do not do what I want, but I do the very thing I hate,"[67] he was describing Israel under the law. He was using the rhetorical first person "I" to describe Israel's struggle with sin under the law. The law was good in that it drew Israel to the one true living God, but the law imprisoned Israel in sin. The Torah, the law, was never the enemy. Sin was the slave-driver keeping Israel in slavery. Jesus the Messiah sets Israel free from the slavery of sin. Paul repeats this fact in Romans 8:1-4. Jesus is the liberator, but the freeing of sin is in the context of the renewed, redefined people of God. Paul writes, "God's love has been poured into our hearts through the Holy Spirit

---

[65] Romans 7:6

[66] Wright, 1008

[67] Romans 7:15

who has been given to us."[68] The plural pronouns denote the context of Christian community. God showed his love for *us*. Christ died for *us*. *We* have been justified. *We* will be saved from the wrath (judgment) of God. Death and sin have reigned, but in the renewed promise land, grace and life reign through Jesus the Messiah. This movement from death to life is through the Red Sea crossing of baptism.[69]

Sin has, at long last, been condemned in the death of the Messiah. As Paul puts it: "For God has done what the law, weakened by the flesh, could not do. By sending his own Son in the likeness of sinful flesh and for sin, he condemned sin in the flesh."[70] According to Wright, "*This is the divine purpose: that sin be drawn onto this one place, onto Israel, so that it can be dealt with conclusively by the covenant God himself in the person, in the flesh of Israel's Messiah, the son of this very God.*"[71] So what was the point of creating Israel as a chosen people and giving them the law? Wright answers: "*The point of Israel's election was not 'for the creator God to have a favourite people' but for the sin of Adam to be dealt with. Election itself, and Torah as the gift which sealed election, was designed—this is Paul's point—to draw sin onto that one place so that it could be successfully condemned right there.*"[72] God's act of election reveals his desire to rescue all of humanity suffering under the cruel oppression of sin.

In Romans 8, Paul turned his attention to the newly defined people of God as the new temple where God's Spirit dwells, a people led by the Spirit, just as the people of Israel were led by a

---

[68] Romans 5:5

[69] See Romans 6:3-4

[70] Romans 8:3

[71] Wright, 1015

[72] Wright, 1015

pillar of cloud by day and a pillar of cloud by night. Paul writes, "The Spirit himself bears witness with our spirit that we are children of God."[73] The Spirit redefines the children of God as those who have been incorporated in Jesus the Messiah. The world-wide implications of the demonstration of God's covenant faithfulness is experienced by creation itself in the rhetorical climax of Romans 8, where Paul writes, "For the creation waits with eager longing for the revealing of the sons of God. For the creation was subjected to futility…(creation waits to) obtain the freedom of the glory of the children of God."[74] In the end, the Creator's action of putting humanity right opens the door for God to make right the entirety of his good creation.

[73] Romans 8:16
[74] Romans 8:19-21

CHAPTER 6

GOD'S FUTURE: ESCHATOLOGY REIMAGINED

Paul and the Faithfulness of God, Chapters 11

The fascinating topic of eschatology, the study of God's future for God's world, is not the caboose at the end of the train; it is the engine driving the entire theological enterprise. The fuel of eschatology is hope. According to Wright: "*Many ancient Jews clung on to a hope which had specific content and shape. Rooted in scripture, this was a hope not just for an individual future after death, but for a restoration and renewal of the whole nation, and perhaps even for the entire created order.*"[1] Paul connected eschatology to both election and monotheism. Jewish hope was never an isolated, individual hope, but the hope that the one true God has a redemptive plan for the entire world. In Wright's words, Paul's hope was "*not simply a*

---

[1] Wright, 1043

hope beyond the world. It is a hope for the world."[2] Paul held on to a Jewish hope reimagined in light of Jesus the Messiah who had come, marking the return of Yahweh to Zion. Messiah had come and he will come again, making Paul's hope somewhat complex. For Paul, God's future plan had begun (Christ has come), but it was not complete (Christ will come again). The present time was in between "the already" and the "not yet" of the day of the Lord. During this time those who are in Messiah experience transformation of character, becoming people fit for the age to come. Jewish hope was built around the return of Yahweh to Zion where he would rule and sort out everything that had gone wrong, which is what Paul meant by judgment. The coming of Jesus and the Spirit meant Yahweh had already returned, but the future coming of Jesus implied Yahweh's return was still not yet.

According to Wright: *"What Yahweh does in the tabernacle or temple is a sign and foretaste of what he intends to do in and for the whole creation...to fill the whole earth with his glory and to set up his kingdom of justice, peace and prosperity."*[3] This rule through the coming of Messiah would show God's faithfulness to his covenant (i.e. his righteousness) and therefore enable his people to "bless the families of the earth" and "inherit the world." This coming rule, the age to come, has broken into this present world dominated by sin and death. We who are in the body of Messiah have received eternal life, that is, the life of the age to come.

Hope Reimagined by Jesus and the Spirit

The resurrection of Jesus the Messiah marked a definite breaking in of the age to come into this present evil age. Paul writes, "But in fact

[2] Wright, 1044
[3] Wright, 1053

Christ has been raised from the dead, the firstfruits of those who have fallen asleep."[4] The presence of the age to come marked by the resurrection of Jesus is kingdom-language. The age to come has been escorted in by the kingdom of God. "Then comes the end," according to Paul, "when he delivers the kingdom to God the Father after destroying every rule and every authority and power. For he must reign until he has put all his enemies under his feet. The last enemy to be destroyed is death."[5] So we are not waiting for Jesus to rule. Paul makes it clear: Jesus is already, presently, ruling as the world's true Lord and King. His rule has begun but it is not complete and the rule of King Jesus is undoubtedly political in nature: "*When Paul said that Jesus was now in charge, he meant something much more dangerous and subversive. He meant, in some sense or other, that Caesar was not the world's ultimate ruler.*"[6] Calling Jesus "King" and "Lord" implies the kingdom had come to overthrow the current structures of political authority, which was the very hope of Jewish eschatology. As we change our allegiance from the kingdom of the world to the kingdom of God, we are freed from the captivity of the present evil age. Paul writes, "(Jesus) gave himself for our sins to deliver us from the present evil age, according to the will of our God and Father"[7] to which Wright adds: "*The 'evil of the present age,' in Jewish thought, consists not in the present world being a dark, wicked place from which we should try to escape, but in the intrusion into, and infection of, God's good creation with the power of evil.*"[8]

---

[4] 1 Corinthians 15:20

[5] 1 Corinthians 15:24-26

[6] Wright, 1065

[7] Galatians 1:4

[8] Wright, 1069

We have been delivered from the present evil age as the new-exodus people of God. We were slaves to sin and subject to death, but now we have been liberated and brought to the promised land where we have received the life of the age to come. This new exodus fits squarely with Jewish expectations, although reimagined by the cross and resurrection of Messiah. Shockingly, Jesus as the new Moses brought about our liberation by his death at the hands of the very authorities he was overthrowing. Any talk of the atonement, which is the meaning and implications of the death of Jesus, needs to consider this historical context of the death of Messiah. For Wright: *"The cross, then, is not simply part of the definition of God or the key fulcrum around which the purpose of God in election is accomplished. It is also at the heart of Paul's inaugurated eschatology."*[9] An "inaugurated eschatology" implies the launching of God's new creation project. The death of Jesus, as the means by which the new age breaks into the old, demonstrates and brings God's future into the present.

We who are in Messiah are the new temple where the Spirit dwells. The Holy Spirit accomplishes the work of heart-transformation, the circumcision of the heart, a sign that Yahweh has returned to his people.[10] We wait with all creation for the grand reworking and renewal of all things and the Spirit has been given to us as a deposit "the guarantee of our inheritance until we acquire possession of it."[11] Wright calls Paul's vision of the future: *"Spirit-driven inaugurated eschatology."*[12] New creation has begun in us by the Holy Spirit as a sign of what is to come.

[9] Wright, 1071

[10] See Romans 2:28-29

[11] Ephesians 1:14

[12] Wright, 1078

The Day of the Lord

The day of the Yahweh has become the day of our Lord Jesus. As we have seen, that day has come and is coming. Paul writes: "...who will sustain you to the end, guiltless in the day of our Lord Jesus Christ."[13] This day will be a time of judgment, not simply condemnation. On that day, the creator God will sort things out and make right everything that is out of order. This day will mark the appearing of Jesus. It is not so much that he will come back as if he has been far away. Rather he will appear, meaning he has always been present, and on that day he will make his presence known.

The day of the Lord will unveil the wrath of God, judgment for people with hard, unrepentant hearts who have been storing up judgment for themselves.[14] God will ultimately rid the world of evil and renew and restore all creation. The creator God, the one God of Israel appearing in the person of the Messiah, made a world fit for himself and he shall restore it and fill it with his own presence and justice.

Eschatology and Ethics

According to Wright, "*The new world beckons.*"[15] The world of new creation under the rule of King Jesus and made known within us by the Spirit calls to us and invites us to live a certain way, distinctly different from those who live in the world dominated by sin and death. Protestant Christianity has a tendency to push ethics to the background and pull salvation to the foreground in fear of equating

---

[13] 1 Corinthians 1:8, see also 1 Corinthians 5:5; 2 Corinthians 1:14; 1 Thessalonians 5:2; 2 Thessalonians 2:2

[14] See Romans 2:5

[15] Wright, 1096

ethics with "works." The danger seen by those with a strong Reformed impulse is people will attempt to earn their salvation by works if ethics are too close to the center of Paul's theology. However Wright argues: *"Once we understand how Paul's eschatology works, and how moral behaviour and indeed moral effort (a major theme in Paul, screened out altogether within some interpretative traditions) is reconceived within that world, any such imagined danger disappears."*[16]

Paul binds together his particular set of ethics with his eschatology. We who are in Messiah have the responsibility of cooperating with the creator God in his new creation project and so God is developing within us the kind of character necessary to be up for the task. Paul did not work out a sophisticated theology out of Jewish story and symbols and then merely add a few unrelated moral commands. Paul's ethics go hand-in-hand with his theological vision of the arrival of new creation, as if he is proclaiming: "The kingdom has come. Yahweh has returned to make everything new and put everything back into order. This is big news! This changes everything! We cannot live the way we used to live!" In the body of Messiah we are a new humanity living in a Spirit-breathed, Spirit-formed new creation. We are not simply imitating what we have seen Jesus do; rather we are living out of a new identity made real by the Spirit. According to Wright, we are cooperating with the Spirit: *"Part of the mystery of the spirit's work, at least as Paul understands its work, is that work does not cancel out human moral effort, including thought, will, decision and action. Rather, it makes them all possible. It opens up a new kind of freedom..."*[17] As Jesus the Messiah has fulfilled the Torah, so those who are in Messiah and walk by the Spirit are fulfilling the Torah as well.

---

[16] Wright, 1097

[17] Wright, 1106-1107

Those in the body of Messiah have indeed received the life of the age to come and are already participating in that age, but the new age is not yet here in its fullness. It has officially been launched but it is not complete. Those in Messiah are pushing towards the finish line: *"Chasing towards the line: one of Paul's various athletic metaphors, indicating that the 'not yet' of eschatology does not mean hanging around with nothing to do."*[18] Messiah's people are pressing toward the goal, running towards the finish line in Wright's words, in order to become fully mature, fully transformed into Christ-likeness. We push towards those things, admitting we have not yet arrived. Paul writes: "For you may be sure of this, that everyone who is sexually immoral or impure, or who is covetous (that is, an idolater), has no inheritance in the kingdom of Christ and God. Let no one deceive you with empty words, for because of these things the wrath of God comes upon the sons of disobedience. Therefore do not become partners with them; for at one time you were darkness, but now you are light in the Lord. Walk as children of light."[19] In other words, Paul warns that those who live in the darkness of the present evil age will not inherit the kingdom of God. Those who are living in the light of the age to come should not partner with them. They are living in the not yet. We are living in the age that has already come. For Wright: *"Paul envisions a renewed humanity in terms of new creation, a new world in which the creator's original intention would at last be fulfilled; and this new world is to be seen in advance in the Messiah's people....Sexual immorality destroys the vision of new creation in which the purpose begun in Genesis 1 and 2 can at last find fulfillment."*[20]

[18] Wright, 1113

[19] Ephesians 5:5-8

[20] Wright, 1117

The way we live in the present evil age anticipating the age to come is the way of love: *"Love, then, is obviously and uncontroversially central to Paul's vision of the Christian moral life, in a way not true in either Judaism or the greco-roman world."*[21] Love flows from a transformed character and a renewed mind. Christians belonging to Messiah develop and maintain Christian patterns of thinking. For Paul, the human mind is able to grasp key truths about the creator God, which guides behavior. The mind and heart are not divided in Paul's theology.

How does Israel factor into God's future? Wright answers with an appeal to the work of the Messiah: *"If Jesus really was Israel's Messiah, as (the first Christians) believed the resurrection had demonstrated him to be, then in some sense or other the narrative and identity of Israel had not been 'replaced' but fulfilled — fulfilled by him in person, and therefore fulfilled in and for all his people."*[22] In Galatians, Paul describes the people of God as once enslaved by sin to the Torah, but now "no longer a slave, but a son, and if a son, then an heir through God."[23] He chose Hagar and Sarah as examples of two different ways of being the people of God. Hagar, the mother of Ishmael, was from Mount Sinai representing the law given to Moses. Sarah, the mother of Isaac, represented the promise given to Abraham. By faith, and not by the Torah, the people of Messiah are children of the promise. Therefore, Paul writes, "For freedom Christ has set us free; stand firm therefore, and do not submit again to a yoke of slavery."[24] The purpose for Paul's metaphor was neither to parse out the differences between Judaism

[21] Wright, 1119
[22] Wright, 1129
[23] Galatians 4:7
[24] Galatians 5:1

and Christianity nor describe how an individual is saved. The issue at the heart of this metaphor was this: How does the life, death, and resurrection of Jesus shape how we are to be the people of God in the age to come? Paul writes: "For through the Spirit, by faith, we ourselves eagerly wait for the hope of righteousness. For in Christ Jesus neither circumcision nor uncircumcision counts for anything, but only faith working through love."[25] As we wait in hope, all that matters for Jews and Gentiles is living out our common faith in Messiah by gracious acts of love towards God and one another.

Asking questions about Israel brings up questions about being the people of God. In the Messiah, being the people of God has been redefined from slavery under the Torah to freedom by faith and love. Jewish ethnicity and adherence to the Torah are no longer the markers of the people of God. Faith and love now identifies people as God's people. Paul sums up his thoughts at the end of his letter to the Galatians: "For neither circumcision counts for anything, nor uncircumcision, but a new creation. And as for all who walk by this rule, peace and mercy be upon them, and upon the Israel of God."[26] When Paul uses the word "Israel," here he means the people of God, both Jews and Gentiles.

Approaching Difficult Terrain

Paul provides a fuller answer to the question of Israel's role in God's future in Romans 9-11 in perhaps some of the most difficult and complex sections in all of his letters. Wright admits: "*It is easy to be overwhelmed by Romans 9-11: its scale and scope, the mass of secondary literature, the controversial theological and also political topics, and the*

---

[25] Galatians 5:5-6

[26] Galatians 6:15-16

huge and difficult questions of the overall flow of thought on the one hand and the complex details of exegesis and interpretation on the other."[27] We approach Romans 9-11 admitting the difficulty of the challenge before us. Those who say Romans 9-11 is easy to understand and easily applied to our lives have not taken the time to seriously read these 90 verses. Wright discusses this section in the context of eschatology, but these three chapters are connected to monotheism and election, and belong to the rest of Paul's letter to the church in Rome. These chapters are *"bound into the letter's whole structure by a thousand silken strands."*[28]

Romans 9 is filled with questions related to God's future purposes, but this chapter is also a retelling of Israel's story from God's election of them for a specific job to the exodus event with Moses and Pharaoh, including some comments from the prophets. This section follows logically from where Paul left off in Romans 8, where he has discussed the life and love experienced by those who are in the Messiah. Romans 9 deals with those who have not believed, primarily those of Israel who have not believed in Jesus the Messiah.

A helpful tool in understanding this section is to see the structure and counterbalance of the ideas presented with the central thought found in Romans 10:9. Wright outlines the structure like this:

[27] Wright, 1156
[28] Wright, 1157

9:1-5
Heartfelt appeal

11:33-36
Heartfelt doxology

9:6-29
Israel's history

11:1-32
Israel's future

9:30-33
Gentile inclusion/
 Jewish stumbling

10:18-21
Gentile inclusion/
Jewish mercy

10:1-4
Jewish unbelief/
ignorance

10:14-17
Faith/knowledge
of the gospel

10:5-13
The law and the prophets pointing
to covenant renewal

10:9
The gospel: Jesus is Lord

Starting in the Middle: Romans 10:1-17

In quoting from Deuteronomy 30 in Romans 10:6-8, Paul used language to describe the renewal of the covenant and the end of exile. The "righteousness based on faith"[1] is a picture of the faith-based covenant. Deuteronomy 30 contains a commandment which was not in heaven or beyond the sea, but in the mouth and circumcised-hearts of God's people so they can obey. In Romans 10, Paul locates the word in a person's mouth and heart. This word, this message, is the gospel: "If you confess with your mouth that Jesus is Lord and believe in your heart that God raised him from the dead, you will be saved."[2] Paul is still talking about justification, that is the declaration of the one God (rethought monotheism) of those who are in the right as members of the one covenant people (redefined election), a future act declared by God in the present (reimagined eschatology). Jewish people were seeking to establish their own covenant membership in the Jewish law, but justification and salvation were not only for those of Jewish ethnicity. The salvation of Yahweh was for both Jew and Greek alike.[3] Jesus the Messiah was the end, the termination point, of the Torah, making covenant membership available to those who wear the badge of faith. The God of Israel intended on circumcising the hearts of his people according to Deuteronomy 30:6 so, in Wright's words, there would be a "*new way of doing the law.*"[4] According to Paul, preaching becomes necessary in this new way. Preaching the gospel was the announcement that the one God of Jews and Gentiles has become Messiah and King in and through Jesus. Salvation, in

---

[1] Romans 10:6

[2] Romans 10:9

[3] See Romans 10:12-13

[4] Wright, 1173

addition to justification, is now available for all the people of the earth. Keeping in mind Paul's conclusions in these verses at the center of this section can prevent the reader from getting lost in Paul's longer arguments regarding Israel in Romans 9 and 11.

Taking a Step Back: Romans 9:30-33 and 10:18-21

Paul sums up in the final four verses of Roman 9 the case he has been building in that chapter: God chose Israel to be an example of his righteousness, but they have stumbled because they pursued righteousness, that is, covenant status, not by faith but by the Torah. This line of thinking takes us further back to Romans 7 and 8. The Torah gives sin an opportunity to spread, but God condemns sin in the flesh of Jesus the Messiah. Romans 9 describes the election of Israel and their stumbling, but there is no mention of sin, even though Roman 1-8 deals often with the subject of sin. In pursuing a covenant status formed by the Torah, Israel ends up stumbling over the very intent of the law and ultimately the revelation of the Messiah. The Jewish stumbling described in Romans 9:30-33 intended to make the Gentiles jealous as described in Romans 10:18-21. Paul draws upon Moses and Isaiah as witnesses to the intent of the God of Israel to stir up Israel's jealousy in welcoming Gentiles into the covenant.[5] God has not closed himself to Israel. He still holds out his hands of mercy towards them.[6]

---

[5] See Romans 10:19-20

[6] Romans 10:21

Israel's Strange Purpose: Romans 9:6-29

According to Wright, this section is a retelling of the story of Israel beginning with Abraham: *"This, in fact, is how (second-temple Jewish) eschatology works: first you tell the story of Israel so far, and then you look on to what is still to come."*[7] Paul is describing eschatology, but Jewish eschatology deals not only with the future but it includes a recounting of God's activity in the past. In one sense, we could read Romans 9 as describing the past, Romans 10 as dealing with the present, and Romans 11 as Paul's discussion of the future. In Romans 9 Paul is recounting Israel's story and pointing to Israel's Messiah who does for them what they could not do for themselves. The God of Israel has been active in history "showing mercy" and "hardening" in order to fulfill his purposes. Paul is not retelling Israel's history to demonstrate how God saves people using Israel as an example. Rather, Paul is describing God's action in and surrounding Israel, because it is through Israel in particular that God has chosen to save the world.

Paul retells the story of Israel's election from a Jewish point of view. He emphasizes to Gentile believers in Jesus the Messiah that they have been included in the irreplaceable story of God's purposes in and through Israel. God has shown mercy to Jacob (i.e. Israel) in spite of Israel's lack of commitment to the Torah. If God can, by his grace, choose a people unfaithful to the Torah then what if God has chosen to be patient with Gentiles, these seemingly "vessels of wrath"?[8] Paul uses the metaphor of a potter and clay to describe his dealings specifically with Israel and not all humanity. Israel cannot tell God: "You are unfair in molding us in a certain way!" God has chosen Israel and he is the master potter

---

[7] Wright, 1181

[8] Romans 9:22

and can mold pottery in any way he chooses. God's act of choosing for a specific purpose is what Paul means by election: "*It is not, then, that 'election' simply involves a selection of some and a leaving of others, a 'loving' of some and a 'hating' of others. It is that the 'elect' themselves are elect in order to be the place where and the means by which God's redemptive purposes are worked out.*"[9]

God's act of hardening, like his act of electing, demonstrates his saving purposes. Paul writes: "What if God, desiring to show his wrath and to make known his power, has endured with much patience vessels of wrath prepared for destruction, in order to make known the riches of his glory for vessels of mercy, which he has prepared beforehand for glory— even us whom he has called, not from the Jews only but also from the Gentiles?"[10] By writing "what if" Paul introduces a new interpretation to Israel's story. What if God wanted to demonstrate his judgment (wrath) and power (authority) by showing patience towards "vessels of wrath" and revealing the richness of his love in his "vessels of mercy" which includes Gentiles? Paul's readers find their answer in the Messiah. Paul quotes from the prophet Hosea to answer the question: "Those who were not my people I will call 'my people,' and her who was not beloved I will call 'beloved.'"[11] In Jesus the Messiah, God demonstrates his mercy to those who had been perceived to be vessels of judgment.

---

[9] Wright, 1191

[10] Romans 9:22-24

[11] Romans 9:25, quoted from Hosea 2:23

Israel's Mysterious Future: Romans 11:1-32

Paul asks another rhetorical question in Romans 11: "Has God rejected his people?" He answers: "By no means!"[12] If in Romans 9 Paul recounts Israel's history then the counter-balance is an account of Israel's future in Romans 11. Israel has been seemingly "cast away" for a purpose, which would ultimately lead to their acceptance. The inclusion of Gentiles was not a sign indicating the God of Israel has rejected his people; rather it was to make Israel jealous. God has invited Israel to join Gentiles and participate in the reconciliation found in Jesus the Messiah. Paul writes, "For if their rejection [casting away] means the reconciliation of the world, what will their acceptance mean but life from the dead?"[13] The covenant has been renewed for the Jewish people who have come alive in confessing Jesus is Lord. They are experiencing a "partial hardening"[14] not because God has rejected them and replaced them with Gentiles, but so they would become jealous by the Gentile inclusion and all Israel would be saved. Israel stumbled[15], was broken off[16], hardened[17], and "they too have now been disobedient in order that by the mercy shown to you (Gentiles) they also may now receive mercy."[18]

The large, looming question regarding Israel and eschatology remains. Will Israel enter God's salvation? Paul's answer is complex at first glance. In Romans 11:14 Paul expects "some" to be saved,

---

[12] Romans 11:1

[13] Romans 11:15

[14] Romans 11:25

[15] Romans 11:11

[16] Romans 11:19

[17] Romans 11:25

[18] Romans 11:31

but in Romans 11:26 he indicates "all Israel will be saved." Paul does make one thing clear: "God has consigned all to disobedience, that he may have mercy on all."[19] God's mercy extends to all, Jew and Gentile alike, but will all Israel be saved or just some? We find the answer by looking back at the rhetorical center of Romans 9-11, which is in the heart of this section: "...If you confess with your mouth that Jesus is Lord and believe in your heart that God raised him from the dead, you will be saved. For with the heart one believes and is justified, and with the mouth one confesses and is saved. For the Scripture says, 'Everyone who believes in him will not be put to shame.' For there is no distinction between Jew and Greek; for the same Lord is Lord of all, bestowing his riches on all who call on him. For 'everyone who calls on the name of the Lord will be saved.'"[20] Jews cannot boast and neither can Gentiles, because Jesus is Lord of both. Gentiles have been grafted in and if Jews have been broken off, God has the power to graft them in again. Salvation for Israel is the same as salvation for the Gentile nations; it is found in a covenant status pursued by faith in Jesus the Messiah.

The Beginning and the End: Romans 9:1-5 and Romans 11:33-36

These two sections together follow the pattern of many of the Psalms, by opening with a lament and closing with praise. Paul opens with: "I have great sorrow and unceasing anguish in my heart. For I could wish that I myself were accursed and cut off from Christ for the sake of my brothers, my kinsmen according to the

[19] Romans 11:32
[20] Romans 10:9-13

flesh."[21] He closes this section with: "For from him and through him and to him are all things. To him be glory forever. Amen."[22] According to Wright: *"Paul is doing again what he does best: expounding the ancient faith of Israel, rethought and reimagined around Jesus and the spirit, in such a way as to take every thought captive to obey the Messiah."*[23]

Summing Up Paul's Theology

Paul has taken three Jewish themes—monotheism, election, and eschatology—and thoroughly reworked them in light of Jesus the Messiah and the coming of the Spirit. In doing so he has transformed the hope of Israel by bringing the Jewish law to its intended termination point. The covenant has been renewed as promised. Yahweh has been faithful to the covenant and has returned to his people who are marked by faith in the Messiah. His Spirit now dwells in his rebuilt temple, that temple made with stones that breathe. His final act of judgment has been experienced by those in the body of Messiah. Both Jews and Gentiles have been declared in the right and thus members of God's covenant family. God's action of blessing, saving, and healing the world has begun, but it is not complete. God has been faithful to his promise to Abraham, faithful to the covenant that has been displayed by the faithfulness of Jesus the Messiah.

---

[21] Romans 9:2-3

[22] Romans 11:36

[23] Wright, 1256

CHAPTER 7

PAUL IN HISTORY

Paul and the Faithfulness of God, Chapters 12-16

N. T. Wright has taken us into Paul's world, particularly the world of pagan religion, Greek philosophy, and Roman politics. We have seen Paul's Jewish context and his Jewish worldview, two things which formed the foundation for a detailed examination of his theology summarized by monotheism, election, and eschatology. These three Jewish concepts were massively rethought and reworked by him in light of the coming of Jesus the Messiah and the coming of the Spirit. Now Wright wants to bring it all back home with an exploration of Paul's theology at work in Paul's world with a spotlight on:

1. Paul in the politics of the Roman Empire
2. Paul in the world of religion
3. Paul and the philosophers
4. Paul in his native Jewish world.

Paul and Caesar

"Every step Paul took, he walked on land ruled by Caesar."[1] The
language Paul used to talk about Jesus did not derive *from* the
empire; it was a direct confrontation *to* the empire. Paul expected
the Jewish Messiah to judge the nations and bring salvation and
peace to the world. The nations had their leaders, but this
arrangement was temporary. Paul preached the gospel of Jesus as
Israel's Messiah and the world's true King which created
communities loyal to Jesus as Lord, Savior, and Son of God, titles
already used in the empire to speak of the Caesar. Paul encouraged a
respect for those in authority, but the idolatry and arrogance of
Caesar was challenged by these communities who reserved their
deepest loyalties for Jesus the Messiah. Paul does not proclaim Jesus
as a better version of Caesar; rather the gospel of Jesus subverts and
overtakes the gospel of Caesar. According to Wright, *"In a world
where loyalty to Caesar had become one of the major features of life, it
could be that the Christians were 'working out their own salvation with
fear and trembling', and coming to realize that, somehow or other, if
Jesus was lord Caesar was not."*[2]

Paul did not endorse the Roman way, but he did call for
submission to Roman authority as a way to live wisely in the
empire. Followers of Messiah in these scattered communities of
faith respected those in civic authority knowing ruling authorities
are ultimately held accountable by Jesus the final judge and supreme
ruler. Earthly rulers will stand before the judge as will all people.
Paul advocated a different kind of politic centered in and around
the Messiah which created a certain kind of revolution, but not the
kind that separated Messiah's people from the greater culture.

[1] Wright, 1271

[2] Wright, 1302

Wright envisions this revolution as a subversive one: *"(Paul) saw the gospel of Jesus the Messiah as upstaging, outflanking, delegitimizing and generally subverting the 'gospel' of Caesar and Rome."*[3] Living as loyal subjects of the Messiah did not require, in Wright's words, either *"Constantinian compromise"* or *"Anabaptist detachment,"* but rather a visible witness to a *"gospel-shaped and gospel revealed new world of justice and peace."*[4]

Paul and Pagan Religion

Religion in the world of Paul did not teach people how to behave as much as it provided signs, myths, and rituals binding people together. The use of Jewish Scriptures and the worship of one God would have seemed strange to pagan onlookers. Yet it was the one God of Israel, one Lord Jesus, and one Spirit that bound together the followers of Jesus the Messiah. These communities had a unique way of talking about God and a unique set of rituals. Baptism as the initiation into the Christian community and the celebration of the Eucharist formed the primary rituals for Paul's communities: *"The eucharist thus clearly functions for Paul as a rite, complete with traditional words; as a rite in which a 'founding myth' was rehearsed, though in this case the founding myth' was an actual event which had occurred not long before; as a rite in which the worshippers share the life of the divinity being worshipped, though the divinity in question is a human being of recent memory; as a rite dependent on a prior sacrifice, albeit the very strange one of the crucifixion of that same human being; as a rite which should bind the community together...."*[5] These practices would have looked like a

---

[3] Wright, 1306

[4] Wright, 1318

[5] Wright, 1347-1348

religion, but one the world had never seen before. It had all the marks of ancient religion but it was infused with theology in a new and unique way.

Paul and Philosophy

The Jesus Paul preached embodied the beauty of truth. According to Wright: *"Jesus is not simply one person whom one might know certain things. He is the one in whom the very treasures of knowledge itself are hidden."*[6] Greek philosophers were interested in three topics: logic (what we know), physics (what there is), and ethics (what we do). In the Greek mind, theology was a subset of physics, but Paul challenged such a view as the God of Israel was not a thing in the material universe.

Regarding questions of logic, Paul would argue, in Wright's words, *"there is a deeper darkness and a new dawn"* regarding human knowledge.[7] Greek philosophy was about coming out of the darkness in order to see what others could not see, but Paul argued for a deeper darkness. He wrote to the Ephesians describing Gentiles who were "darkened in their understanding."[8] They lived in darkness as they have lived lives with distorted habits of behavior rooted in a hardness of heart, the result of humanity going terribly wrong as described in Genesis 3-11. Jesus as the light of the world has provided the true light, illuminating even the deepest darkness of the human heart.

Regarding questions of physics, Paul steadfastly remained a creational monotheist. The God of Israel has created all things through Jesus the Messiah. Paul writes, "All things were created

[6] Wright, 1361
[7] Wright, 1362
[8] Ephesians 4:18

through him and for him."[9] Even in their darkness, humanity can see God's divine attributes in creation, but because they remain in darkness the light of the one God is necessary to see all things as they are. As the creator, God will ultimately call all things into account.

Regarding questions of ethics, the dominant logic of the Greek philosophers was once humanity can discover what is out there, they should then go with the grain of the way things are. The Stoics saw divinity in everything, so right living was a matter of going along with the natural course of things. The Epicureans saw the gods as far away, but admitted the gods set up things before their departure, so, like the Stoics, humanity should just go with the flow of life. In stark contrast, Paul's ethics were tied not to the ways things are, but to eschatology, how things will be under the reign of Messiah. Paul's inaugurated eschatology announced the coming of the light of truth, beauty, and goodness. Therefore, with the dawn of the Messiah, the people of Messiah should live in the light of this new world, the one that has come and is coming. According to Wright, *"Paul believed that the world had been renewed in the Messiah; that those who were themselves 'in the Messiah' had also been renewed as image-bearing human beings; and that the task of such people was to live in accordance with the new world, rather than against its grain."*[10] The arrival of God's new world marked the power of the gospel to make humanity truly human again.

Paul and His Jewish Context

For Wright, Paul was undoubtedly an apostle to the Gentile nations sent as a Jewish thinker: *"He came with a Jewish message and a Jewish*

[9] Colossians 1:16
[10] Wright, 1371

way of life for the non-Jewish world. He did not see himself as founding or establishing a new, non-Jewish movement. He believed that the message and life he proclaimed and inculcated was, in some sense, the fulfillment of all he had believed as a strict Pharisaic Jew."[11] Paul was a Jew by birth and he had no modern notions of converting to another religion. He did not compare religions or offer something in the Messiah to replace religion in general or the Jewish religion in particular. He was not attempting to start anything new or replace religion with something called "faith." He was extending to non-Jews the opportunity of membership in the renewed-covenant with the God of Israel. Paul did have an encounter with Jesus the Messiah which solidified his call and it became the impetus towards rethinking and reimagining what it meant to be a Jew. Paul admitted he died to the law. He had been crucified and raised with the Messiah. His identity was no longer Jewish but *Messiah-ish*. Paul was ethnically a Jew but ethnicity was no longer his primary identity. In Messiah, Paul found his true identity and from that place he called people to imitate him as he imitated the Messiah as he was enabled by the Spirit.

Paul was a reader of Israel's scripture and he did not randomly pick verses from the Jewish scripture in order to make them fit what he was writing. Paul was well aware of the context of the specific verses he quoted. The larger context was on his mind when he used particular quotations from the Old Testament. He understood the tension present in the Old Testament between the promise of God and the commands of God, that is, the promise to bless, save, and redeem the world through the people of Abraham on one hand and the system of blessings and curses in the Torah based on Israel's response to the covenant on the other hand. This tension seemed

---

[11] Wright, 1408

like "two voices" or "two movements" in Israel's narrative history. Nevertheless, the entirety of Jewish thought, including the Jewish scriptures, was, for Paul rethought, redefined, and reimagined in light of the coming of Jesus the Messiah and the Spirit.

In reading and using Old Testament scripture in his writings, Paul is reworking it in the larger context of Israel's narrative history: *"Paul reads Israel's scriptures as a vast and complex narrative, the story of the faithful creator, the faithful covenant God, the god who in Israel's Messiah kept his ancient promises and thereby created a people marked out by their pistis, their own gospel-generated faith or faithfulness. The scriptures do not so much bear witness, for Paul, to an abstract truth ('the one God is faithful'). They narrate that faithfulness, and in doing so, invite the whole world into the faithful family whose source and focus is the crucified and risen Messiah."*[12]

Paul's Primary Purpose

Wright draws upon the words of Jewish political theorist, Hannah Arendt, to describe the Jewish desire to move in action in the present. He quotes Arendt who wrote: "We can no longer afford to take that which was good in the past and simply call it our heritage, to discard the bad and simply think of it as a dead load which by itself time will bury in oblivion. The subterranean stream of Western history has finally come to the surface and usurped the dignity of our tradition. This is the reality in which we live. And this is why all efforts to escape from the grimness of the present into nostalgia for a still intact past, or into the anticipated oblivion of a better future, are vain." For Wright: *"The Messiah and the redemption of history...has to do not simply with 'spirituality' or 'religion', not with*

---

[12] Wright, 1471

an escapist salvation in which of the world ceases to matter, but with the challenge to action in the world itself."[13]

This decidedly Jewish impulse towards action in the world was present in Paul. He was not a detached thinker, but a doer. He was a thinker no doubt, but he was not content with merely dreaming up some good ideas and talking about them. The God of Israel had returned to his people. Messiah had come and the Spirit of Yahweh was dwelling within the human, flesh and blood, temple of his renewed people, and above all, God's act of new creation had begun! God's action prompted Paul to act. So what was Paul trying to do? Wright's answer is found in the life and vitality of the church: "*Paul's practical aim was the creation and maintenance of particular kinds of communities; that the means to their creation and maintenance was the key notion of reconciliation; and that these communities, which he regarded as the spirit-inhabited Messiah-people, constituted at least in his mind and perhaps also in historical truth a new kind of reality, embodying a new kind of philosophy, of religion and of politics, and a new kind of combination of those; and all of this within the reality we studied in the previous chapter, a new kind of Jewishness, a community of new covenant, a community rooted in a new kind of prayer.*"[14]

Paul did not write philosophical essays or political manifestos; he wrote letters to churches. Paul's aims and intentions were wrapped up in the planting, building, and the flourishing of the local church.[15] Paul's aims or goals can be best described as a ministry of reconciliation. The words "mission" and "evangelism" in our modern

---

[13] Wright, 1474

[14] Wright, 1476

[15] *Paul and the Faithfulness of God* is the fourth in a series of academic books on "Christian origins." According to Wright, his next volume in this series after the Paul book is a book on Christian missiology.

context have departed somewhat from what they meant during the time Paul was planting churches throughout the Mediterranean world of the ancient Roman Empire. Evangelism for Paul was not a matter of "saving souls for heaven," a phrase we never see in Paul's writings, or anywhere in scripture for that matter. When Paul was traveling, preaching, teaching, writing, and suffering on behalf of the church, he saw himself as engaging in the ministry of reconciliation. Wright notes: *"For Paul, everything grew into the field of God's new world."*[16] Those who are in the Messiah have entered into God's new world. Paul writes, "Therefore, if anyone is in Christ [behold] new creation. The old has passed away; behold, the new has come. All this is from God, who through Christ reconciled us to himself and gave us the ministry of reconciliation; that is, in Christ God was reconciling the world to himself, not counting their trespasses against them, and entrusting to us the message of reconciliation."[17] This new world is a world reconciled to God and those who are in Christ are a reconciled people. This new world launched with the resurrection of Jesus is the first stage of the renewal of all creation.

These new communities formed around the Messiah would appear to the outside world to be a new school of philosophy, a new kind of religion, a new political movement heralding a new king and a new way of being human. Wright contends: *"If we do not recognize Paul's churches as in some sense philosophical communities, religious groups and political bodies it is perhaps because we have been thinking of the modern meanings of such terms rather than those which*

[16] Wright, 1488
[17] 2 Corinthians 5:17-19

were known in Paul's world."[18] These reconciled communities were to be a prototype of what is to come, demonstrating to the world what it looked like to be reconciled to one another and to the God of all creation. Paul saw his ministry of reconciliation and the ministry of the church as temple-building and not soul-saving. His mission was to build the communities as mini-temples where the Spirit of Yahweh would dwell. Individuals experienced the Spirit, but each individual reconciled to God, indwelt by God's Spirit, living in God's new world, served as a signpost to a larger truth, namely the faithfulness of God demonstrated in his people for his world. These new temple-communities were made up of Jews and Gentiles living in unity. The gospel Paul preached was for the Jew first but also for a Greek, an unquestionable *"Jewish message for the non-Jewish world."*[19]

Paul would not have seen the modern subjects of theology and politics as separate and unrelated themes. Paul was a Roman citizen, but his allegiance was to the Messiah and his citizenship was in/from heaven. This dual citizenship was consistent with Paul's eschatology. The age to come had broken into history, but it is not here in its fullness. Jesus the Messiah has been highly exalted over all earthly political figures, but Caesar still reigns. We best see the Messiah's reign within the local communities worshipping Jesus the Messiah. Caesar, to some extent, had tried to create such a religion within the empire whereby he would be the object of people's devotion. Caesar's reign over his empire would not endure as long as Jesus' reign through his church.

Not only did Paul see Jesus' reign as superior to the reign of Caesar, he saw, in Wright's words, the reign of Jesus as an *"integrated*

---

[18] Wright, 1492
[19] Wright, 1498

vision of the one God and his world."[20] Paul would agree all truth is God's truth and he regularly affirmed the goodness of creation. God's kingdom in and through the reign of Messiah was a physical, earth-bound kingdom. For Wright, Paul built communities for this world: "*Paul's aim was to be the temple-builder for the kingdom, planting on non-Jewish soil little communities in which heaven and earth would come together at last, places where the returning glory of Israel's god would shine out, heralding and anticipating the day when God would be all in all.*"[21] Paul proclaimed the death and resurrection of Jesus the Messiah and trusted the power of the gospel message to transform the lives of those who received it. Paul's theology was important, but not as stand-alone intellectual speculation. Paul's theology lived and breathed in these gospel-formed communities.

Reconciliation and integration are good ways to sum up Paul's theology. We who study Paul's theology in modern-day communities of our own should expect the reconciliation and integration of those who see justification as primarily God's legal action and those who see justification as primarily God's invitation for us to join him.[22] Our study of Paul should lead to an end to the squabbling between those of the "old perspective" and those of the "new perspective(s)" on Paul. We should hope to see an integration of those who are interested in Paul's historical context with those who are interested in Paul's theological perspective because the Jesus of history is the Christ of faith.

---

[20] Wright, 1508

[21] Wright, 1509

[22] Wright hopes for a coming together of those who read Paul as primarily "juridical" or "forensic" and those who read Paul from a "participationist" point of view.

In the end we, like Paul, are best served when our life of study and participation in the community of faith are sustained by prayer. According to Wright: "*The renewed praise of Paul's doxologies takes its place at the historically situated and theologically explosive fusion of worlds where Paul stood in the middle, between Athens and Jerusalem, between the kingdom of God and the kingdoms of the world, between Philemon and Onesimus, between history and theology, between exegesis and the life of the church, between heaven and earth.*" (1518) Paul is a central figure in Christian theology, because in some sense, he created what we know as Christian theology.

Wright ends the book with these words: "Paul's 'aims', his apostolic vocation, modeled the faithfulness of God. Concentrated and gathered. Prayer became theology, theology prayer. Something understood."[23] Paul's work as an apostle included the writing of letters which we call sacred scripture. He wrote at a particular time in history in a particular culture, but his writings bear the mark of inspiration by the breath of God, the Spirit of God. In seeking to understand Paul's theology preserved for us in scripture, we need the Spirit to guide, direct, and enable our efforts. So we pray along with Paul, "that according to the riches of his glory he may grant you to be strengthened with power through his Spirit in your inner being, so that Christ may dwell in your hearts through faith—that you, being rooted and grounded in love, may have strength to comprehend with all the saints what is the breadth and length and height and depth, and to know the love of Christ that surpasses knowledge, that you may be filled with all the fullness of God."[24] Amen.

---

[23] Wright, 1519

[24] Ephesians 3:16-19

EPILOGUE

Reading, teaching, and now creating a reader's guide for *Paul and the Faithfulness of God* has been an eighteen-month labor of love. On the last night of the class I taught on the book, someone asked me what I had learned. I stumbled over my response. I have read so much from Wright, so I already had a basic understanding of his emphasis and where he was coming from. Reading the big book on Paul did not serve as a massive paradigm shift for me. It did, however, clarify Paul's use of the concept of election, particularly in Romans 9, an important concept in Paul that I have wrestled with for years. As with many of Wright's books, I grew in my love for the gospel and the church. I am now ever more committed to serving, leading, instructing, and building the local church to be an alternative, subversive community of faith shining forth the light of the gospel. I did conclude each of my class sessions with "final thoughts" from each section of the book. I suppose these are the things I am taking away from the book. To give a better answer to the question "What did you learn from the book?" I offer this brief response.

Paul and the Faithfulness of God attempts to reconcile theology and history. The predominant modern Protestant interpretation of Paul was based on 16th century issues. Wright wants to revisit Paul in the context of the first century. As Wright has repeated so often, *"We must stop giving nineteenth-century answers to sixteenth-century questions and try to give twenty-first-century answers to first-century questions."*[1] Theology matters and so does history. Theology plus history is good theology. Theology minus history is bad theology. We cannot assume as modern readers that we can simply take the Bible in general, or Paul's writing in particular, the "way it is." We need help understanding the text in its historical context, which is to say Paul's first-century Jewish context. Paul remained a Jewish thinker who communicated to Christian congregations spread out in a pagan world. He may have chosen imagery from either the Roman or Greek world in his writing, but he does so from the position of a Jewish thinker with a Jewish worldview.

Worldview is not what we are looking at, but what we are looking through. Our worldview shapes how we interpret, evaluate, and draw conclusions based on what we see. For Paul, his worldview was thoroughly Jewish reimagined in the light of Jesus the Messiah who has come to save the world: the Jewish world and pagan, Gentile world. Understanding Paul's worldview helps us see Paul's point of view in his theology. Paul worked with Jewish language, Jewish themes, and Jewish metaphors. Israel as the people of God and Torah as God-breathed scripture served as primary themes in Paul's worldview. Paul reveals what Israel and Torah could not do, the one God of Israel did through the coming of Jesus and the Spirit. Everything changed for Paul in the presence of Jesus and the Spirit. The primary Jewish themes of monotheism, election, and eschatology where each rethought, redefined, and reimagined.

Monotheism, the one reign of the one God of Israel, informs Paul's understanding of election — God's one promise to bless the

---

[1] Wright, *Surprised by Scripture*, New York: HarperOne: 2014, 26

world by choosing one people to reflect his glory in his world. The "elect" in Paul's writings refer to the people of God identified by faith who have received the task of being the instruments of salvation, reconciliation, and healing of God's good, but broken world. Election is a matter of vocation, not specifically salvation. We discuss Paul's theology of justification by faith in the context of Paul's redefinition of election around the coming of the Holy Spirit, because justification is God's gracious act of declaring in the right those who are a part of the chosen people of God who carry out God's purposes for God's world. The gospel is for the Jew first and also for the Greek, the Gentile, the non-Jew. The gospel declares how the God worshiped by the Jews has become the King of the world. The future for Israel and Gentile nations depends on how they respond to the gospel. God's future is filled with new creation. This new world has broken into the old world, flooding the darkness of this present evil age with light. We who are Messiah's people are called to live as people of the light. Theology, history, and wrestling with scripture all matter because the God of Israel has been faithful to his covenant. His reign has begun! New creation has begun and we get to participate in it as people of the Messiah as the new temple indwelt by the Spirit.